NAVIGATE

SELLING

THE WAY
PEOPLE
LIKE TO
BUY

D1308865

ISBN: 978-0-9815657-2-9

Contents

Dustin,

This is fantastic! I finally had a chance to sit down and read NAVIGATE *this weekend. You are a terrific writer with an ability to put complex thoughts into simple, easy-to-read statements. You have condensed your wisdom into crisp formulas that are easy to remember and easy to apply.*

I have heard you teach a group of salespeople and was impressed by your presence in front of a group—very natural, at ease, funny, and sincere. Your book has the same tone. Your ideas are believable and easy to understand. The beginning salesperson who is starting out will start on a solid foundation. The veteran salesperson with many years of experience will discover new ideas that will lift him or her to new heights of excellence.

Ever since I heard about you, I knew you were a great salesperson. Ever since I met you, I knew you were a great human being. Ever since I read NAVIGATE, *I know you are a great writer!*

Cordially,
Steve Savage, Coauthor of *Guerrilla Business Secrets*
along with Jay Conrad Levinson

Acknowledgements

Thank you for deciding to take your sales skills to the next level by reading NAVIGATE! A special thanks goes to my wife, Kyah Hillis, who is the best saleswoman that I know. Also, I would like to thank Steve Reiner, Lee McCroskey, Dan Moore, Spencer Hays, Henry Bedford, all the sales managers, and the 150,000+ sales professionals who have helped contribute to the ideas in this book. Thanks to the Navigate editing team (This would not have been possible without you all!). Geoffrey Stone, Cindy Johnstone and the FRP team. The outstanding artwork on the cover was provided by Marshall Roman and remastered by The Purple Turtle (www.tptglobal.com). Much Love goes out to the most amazing friends in the world!: (In no particular order ?) Mat K., Mike Z., Dave S., Rory V., Gary M., Dave B., Emmie Y., Amanda J. "AJ", Joe L., Jeanine P., Marc S., Karen K., Shaun D., Collin T., Waylon H., Damon M., Ali H., Johnny W., Brian and Natalie H., Annie K., Rick S., Phil M., Dan D. and the Georgia boys. Lastly, I would like to thank the best salesman I know, Steve Hillis, for the support and wisdom throughout the years.

Preface

My years in college were a tremendous learning experience for me. Not only did I learn a lot about psychology as I earned my B.A., but I learned a lot about myself and setting goals while working with The Southwestern Company during my summers. I learned that one of the most important traits of a top performer is to never stop learning. Even after college, I wanted to learn more ways to improve my performance. I went through many advanced sales training and self-improvement courses such as navigating the different buying behavior styles called "Selling on Purpose" by Steve Reiner and "Selling Like a Chameleon" by Lee McCroskey. These were selling technique courses held at The Southwestern Company and its sister company, Southwestern Business Resources Consulting. The information from those courses, along with my study of psychology and intense study of personality tests, is the foundation for the Navigate system. These techniques are tried and true—I knocked on ten thousand doors, have called on more than ten thousand top executives and sales professionals across the country, and was able to put this system to the test, with tangible results.

That is the story of how I first learned of the Navigate system, and when I applied it to my approach, this system allowed me to double my productivity. When I began selling books door-to-door, I was treating all potential customers as the same type of buyer. What I learned was, if I changed my words just a little bit (enough to match their buying styles), then within the first seven seconds of contacting them, my success rate doubled. I would connect with them and get in the door twice as many times as before. It caused my business to literally double from one year to the next.

In this book you will learn the method and application of the Navigate system, how it has affected other people's personal production, and how it has made a huge difference in the way they communicate and ask for business. There are four basic buying behavior styles that you need to know in order to be more effective at closing the deal. This book outlines those four buying behavior styles—fighter, entertainer, detective, and counselor—and will show you how to identify the buying styles in others and how to adapt your selling style to best fit the buying style of your customer. Being aware of the different buying behavior styles and knowing how to identify and adapt to the different kinds of decision-makers is key to growing your sales. People buy from people they like and trust. This selling process will enhance your ability to quickly get a person to like you and trust you. Whether you are attempting to set up an appointment, close a deal, or just want someone to hear what you have to say, the Navigate system will help you communicate better and connect with people for the rest of your life!

PART ONE

The Fundamentals

Chapter 1

Connecting with the Buyer

Why can't I connect with this person?

If you have been in sales for any length of time, you probably have asked yourself, "Why can't I connect with this person?" You may have been in a situation where you are on top of your game—presenting all the facts, answering all the objections, and demonstrating the need—but you just haven't been able to make the emotional connection necessary to close the deal. What is it that makes a buyer able to trust you enough to invest in what you are selling? Why are you able to connect so easily with some people and not others? Why does it seem as though your colleague is able to gain the trust of all types of people and close the deal so easily with college kids, parents, businesspeople, and seniors alike? The answer to these questions lies in the buying behavior style of your prospects.

My first sales experience came while I was in college. I was studying psychology at the University of Tennessee. I chose to work my way through school. And I knew the best way to work while in school was to work hard all summer so that I could focus on my classes during the year. That meant I needed a job that would pay well for three months of hard work. That's when I found The Southwestern Company (www.southwestern.com). Southwestern trains college-age adults to sell books door-to-door for a good commission. I had very little selling experience, playing football was all that I knew.

Because I have a competitive nature and a passion for learning new things, I ended up selling books door-to-door for four summers while in college. It was an extraordinary experience. I was working more than eighty hours a week and must have knocked on some twenty-five hundred doors per summer, working on straight commission to pay my way through college. The training at Southwestern is unmatched. After one week of intensive training they took me, an inexperienced college football player, and turned me into a selling machine! After my first summer, I finished number one out of twenty-five hundred first-year sales people. At the end of my second summer, I made a commission check for $46,000—not a bad summer's earnings for a sophomore in college. On one of the last days of that second summer, an experienced salesperson shadowed me. He told me, "If you ever figure out what you are doing, you will break the company record." That comment dumbfounded me. I was already a top producer for the company, and I'm essentially being told that I don't know what I am doing!

That was also the first time the thought entered my mind that maybe I could break the 154-year-old company's sales record. So all during the following year, I studied the psychology of sales. I studied everything: unconditional confidence, social pressure, neurolinguistic programming, and the four different buying behavior styles. I was so intrigued by all of the topics that I started to convert the principles we were being taught at the University of Tennessee and funneling them through a sales-minded filter.

My first mission was to figure out my own behavior style. I took DISC, Myers-Briggs, and any other personality profile test I could find. They were all awesome tests that taught me a lot about myself and my personality, but something was missing. To sell to other personalities, I needed to be able to make the transition from "who I was" to "how I was" selling and more importantly, "who the customer was."

Then in the spring of 2004, I attended a class in Nashville, Tennessee, at The Southwestern Company's headquarters, called "Selling Like a Chameleon." My sales career was changed forever! The program not only identified different buying behavior styles, but it taught me how to adapt my selling style to best match the customer's buying behavior style.

Personality Profiles Versus Buying Behavior Profiles

Personality profile tests, such as Myers-Briggs, are excellent resources for determining one's personality type. A lot of personality tests measure your social personality and how you act and react to a nonthreatening "normal" environment. As we all know, when put in a high-pressure sales/work environment, however, we behave completely differently. It is important to know your own personality type to help you better understand your strengths and weaknesses. This will give you an edge in knowing what tasks you will be better suited to perform and will help you in making decisions about what career path to follow. If you are an analytical achiever, for example, you may find it difficult wooing and relating to people on a deep level. While you could choose a career path that required schmoozing, that wouldn't be where your strengths lie. You would be expending more effort to be merely good at something. Instead, if you chose a career that allowed you to work on analyzing and interpreting data, you might not be improving your interaction skills, but you could become the best data analyst in your field—because that's where your strengths lie. Therefore, personality profile tests are important in giving you a broad picture of yourself, your strengths and weaknesses. Although buying behavior profiles are related to personality tests, they are somewhat different.

Buying behavior profiles look specifically at how a person behaves in a buying situation. Buying behaviors can be different even among similar personality types. For instance, one analytical achiever may approach buying as a fighter, wanting to know the value right away and to get to the point quickly. Another analytical achiever may be the detective, wanting to see the charts and figures that support all the claims and think through all the options. The second scenario is probably more common with an analytical achiever, but it is not necessarily always the case, which is why understanding how to identify and adapt to the different buying behavior styles is so important in becoming a top producer.

The next year I went out with the goal of breaking the company record. That meant more than doubling my production from the prior year. The way to reach my goal was by following the principles learned in the "Selling Like a Chameleon" class and the principles found in this book. ("Selling Like a Chameleon" was a class offered by Southwestern that taught the importance of adapting to different personalities to maximize your sales.) My slight edge for that summer was in my initial contact, the way I approached the buyer. Unlike the previous summers, during my third summer at Southwestern, I tailored my selling style to best match the buyer's behavior styles. During the previous two summers my sales approach had appealed only to people who were like me, so I was connecting with only one-quarter of my prospects. My first two summers, I treated everyone I approached as if he or she were an extroverted entertainer, which is my selling behavior style. I was successful those first two summers in large part because "birds of a feather flock together." The prospects who let me in were extroverts; and they referred me to their friends, who were extroverts; and they referred me to their friends, who were extroverts. You get the picture. However, there are only so many of one type of behavior style in a city. I frequently would run into someone of a different behavior style, and, in those instances, my standard selling style wouldn't work.

When I ran into people with aggressive behavior styles and used the same words I was using with the extroverted people, they were slamming the door in my face! At first I thought it was a problem with them, but after studying the psychology of behavior styles and going through the "Selling Like a Chameleon" course, I came to realize it was a problem with me. After adopting the "Selling Like a Chameleon" approach, my production doubled! As a junior in college, I made more than $100,000 in fourteen weeks! (That was a fun summer.) The exact commission check was $102,000, and I hit my goal of breaking a first-year company selling record!

Emotion Is the Key

Why do people buy things? There are generally two reasons: 1) they want it or they need it; and 2) they like you and trust you. Whatever the case may be, a person typically buys something based on an emotional response. If a person wants something, it is because there is a feeling behind the desire. He or she may think the object will satisfy some need. If a woman wants a new pair of shoes, for example, she may be satisfying a need to look stylish. Her emotions are involved in the buying process. If a person needs something, he will buy it from a source he trusts. Navigate is designed to teach you how to foster an authentic connection with people that creates a genuine feeling of trust.

According to Wikipedia.org, "an emotion is a mental and physiological state associated with a wide variety of feelings, thoughts, and behaviors. It is a prime determinant of the sense of subjective well-being and appears to play a central role in many human activities."

> *We are emotional beings, and our emotions certainly come into play in our buying habits.*

Making a Connection

My dad (Steve) is the most outstanding salesman in the world, and he once told me, "The reason people buy is because they like you and trust you. If you take them to breakfast, you will win the order. If you take them to lunch, you will secure their repeat business. If you can take someone to dinner with his or her significant other, you will have a customer for life!" The key to closing the sale and keeping the customer is to connect with the buyer and develop a deep sense of trust. "The Influence of General Trust and Specific Trust on Buying Behavior," a 2008 article by Peter Kenning, published in the *International Journal of Retail & Distribution Management*, states that of 331 subjects "general as well as specific trust positively affects buying behavior."[2]

> *The key to closing the sale and keeping the customer is to connect with the buyer and develop a deep sense of trust.*

The idea of connecting with the customer is most obviously seen in the vehement way in which top brands protect their image and reputation. In a 2001 Arthur Rock Center for Entrepreneurship interview with Nancy Koehn, author of *Brand New: How Entrepreneurs Earned Consumers' Trust from Wedgwood to Dell* (HBS Press, 2001), Koehn said that "when Michael Dell started out in the PC business, he dealt with many of the firm's potential customers himself. Since he understood that his idea of 'mass customization' depended upon strong connections with his customers, he enlisted knowledgeable, courteous, and responsive salespeople and technicians. Great brand builders have always understood the importance of connecting meaningfully with customers."[3]

Making an emotional connection isn't always easy. Companies will pay millions of dollars to advertising and publicity firms to ensure an emotional connection with customers. Fortune 500 executives and wheelers and dealers spend a lot of time and effort preparing for meetings with key players in order to make a lasting impression and potentially build a valuable relationship. Likewise, top sales producers take note of their customers' body language and verbal communication in order to identify and adapt their selling style to the buying behavior styles of the customer. Becoming a true sales professional and morphing yourself from an order taker to a well-oiled, top-producing machine is not light work, nor does it happen overnight, but this will greatly improve the chance of making a great first impression and a strong emotional connection. It takes a lot of work to learn how to connect with people.

Conclusion

To recap what you have learned, ask yourself:

Why do people buy from you?

- THEY WANT IT
- THEY NEED IT
- THEY LIKE YOU
- THEY TRUST YOU

What is the key to being a top producer?

- MAKING A CONNECTION

How do you make an emotional connection?

- ADAPT YOUR SELLING STYLE
- FIND OUT WHAT THE CUSTOMER IS INTERESTED IN

For your free "Navigate Sales Diagnosis" go to:

http://www.ssnseminars.com/Sales-Coaching.aspx and click on the *chat live* button.

Also join our free e-zine at:

http://members.audiogenerator.com/info.asp?x=137686

Chapter 2

The Sales Cycle

People love to buy, but they hate to be sold.

Execution of the fundamentals and using the techniques in this book are keys to becoming a successful top producer. The core fundamental principles of success must be followed before applying any of the more advanced techniques discussed in part 3. The core fundamental principles to follow are hard work, positive mental attitude, and working like a true professional. You must become a student of the selling game and follow the cycle of the sale. I like to think of the sales cycle as a flowing river that needs to be navigated. That's why this book is called Navigate. Hard work will keep the leads coming. It will open the doors to sales potential. Your positive mental attitude will give you the endurance you need to keep going, even when experiencing rejection. Learning how to work like a true professional is where you can begin to outperform your colleagues by understanding and applying the Navigate techniques of selling to the buyer's buying behavior style. This is how you make the emotional connection needed in order to close more sales!

The core fundamental principles to follow are hard work, positive mental attitude, and working like a true professional.

The sales cycle has been around as long as people have been selling things. There are a number of models out there that are fine. The sales cycle model that I teach and follow myself focuses on techniques and principles that have been proven to work time and time again. It is what I learned back when I was working at Southwestern, when I was one of twenty-five hundred college students working out of state, going door-to-door, to sell educational reference books, software, and CDs to help students save time on homework. Still today our sales consulting team at Success Starts Now!™ (www.ssnseminars.com) uses the same proven tested sales cycle. The successes of Southwestern's 150,000-plus salespeople, and of my record-breaking years knocking on doors, prove that these principles work.

Master "Navigators" and sales professionals know the psychology behind the selling cycle and why it works. It is designed to save time and increase production by following these seven steps:

1. Prospecting /Pre-approach
2. Approach
3. Qualifying/Introduction/Active Listening
4. Presentation
5. Answering Objections or Concerns
6. Closing
7. Referrals/Follow-up

Prospecting/Pre-approach

True business professionals do their homework on a client before they engage in a business discussion. The term pre-approach means the work that is done before the approach. There are four main benefits to the pre-approach:

1. Lets you identify their Navigate buying behavior style.
2. Helps you connect and build instant rapport.
3. Tells you who the decision-maker is.
4. Saves time.

Pre-approach is a simple concept and so beneficial, yet I find many salespeople just pick up the phone and dive right into a good lead or referral without asking any questions about that lead. I don't know if it comes from laziness or just not being aware of the pre-approach concept. The Navigate pre-approach is as simple as asking the following four questions every time you receive a referral or a lead:

1. What is the decision-maker's first name?
2. What kind of decision-maker is he or she?
3. What is this person's cell phone number or direct line?
4. What is the best time to reach this person?

By asking for the decision-maker's first name, you accomplish several different objectives. First, you find out who the actual decision-maker is, way before you engage in a long, drawn-out presentation. Second, you get the first name and use the first name to apply "peer-to-peer" selling, which is having an attitude of equality with your prospect. Peer-to-peer selling involves a mutual respect for one another, as if you were selling to a good friend or sibling. If calling on Bob Jones, a lot of salespeople will, right out of the gate, call the prospect "Mr. Jones." Instantly, they are trying to play catch-up to win their prospect's respect and trust. Bob knows that the salesperson doesn't know him and is on guard for the rest of the conversation. This can all be solved by using just the prospect's first name immediately when you call on him (or her): "Hi. Is this Bob?" Not only does this imply you know who he is, but it also elicits a dialogue, not a monologue.

Finding out your prospect's decision-making style is one of the best ways to identify his or her buying behavior style. Getting this information out of the person giving you the referral is tricky. There is a right way of asking this question and a wrong way. The wrong way is to ask the person giving you the referral, "What kind of decision-maker is Bob?" The right way is to ask, "What kind of guy is Bob? Is he a straight-to-the-point kind of person, does he take his time to make a decision, or is he analytical? Do I need to make sure to use your name? What would you suggest I know about Bob, so I can be prepared?" By jogging the person's memory, you will know what buying behavior style the referral is before you ever engage in your initial approach.

> *Finding out your prospect's decision-making style is one of the best ways to identify his or her buying behavior style.*

Getting your prospect's cell phone number and finding out the best time to call has at least three distinct advantages. First, when you call someone on his cell phone, it implies peer-to-peer selling. Think about it. Who typically calls you on your cell phone? Family, friends, co-workers, and close acquaintances. Second, which phone do you think a top executive or a busy individual is more likely to answer, his cell phone or his office phone? And third, you can send text messages to a cell phone, which, according to recent studies, is the number one way the millenial generation prefers to communicate.

While putting on one of our Success Starts Now! ™ (www.ssnseminars.com) sales training conferences in San Francisco a few years back, I received a referral for the CEO of a large Fortune 100 company to engage in our customized, ongoing sales consulting programs. I called the headquarters and asked to speak with the sales department. The sales rep answered the phone on the first ring, eager to see how he could assist me. I asked who was in charge of the training and coordination of sales training. He replied that the CEO was. So I asked, "What is his first name, when is the best time to reach him, what kind of decision maker is he, and what is his cell phone number?" Then I called him at the time the rep told me was best—when he was on the golf course. I had done my research ahead of time, so when he answered the phone and asked, "How did you get my cell phone number?" I replied, "It's funny that you ask! That's what I want to teach your sales team!" I was able to show him that I knew a little bit about his company and what it needed. He was impressed by the accuracy of my information and set the appointment.

Approach

The approach is the initial contact that you have with your prospective client. The rule of seven, which I'll get into in more detail later, says that we have only seven seconds to make a first impression. That is how small our window is. People make judgments based on your nonverbal clues: the way you dress, even whether you shine your shoes—everything from your handshake to your eye contact—and your verbal clues: the words that you use within the first seven seconds.

Qualifying/Introduction

The introduction is the most important part of the cycle of the sale. There are four objectives to the introduction:

1. You are building rapport and establishing common ground. Typically, the best way of doing so is through the use of "Third Party Selling," discussed later on in this book.

2. You are determining whether he or she is a qualified prospect: Will she benefit from my product or service? Is he the decision-maker? Is this company financially secure? At Success Starts Now!™, we use a consultative approach to our questioning, qualifying, and probing. My business partner, Rory Vaden, created a great consultative questioning technique called C.L.A.S.P.

   Currently: "What is your current situation?" (This creates a dialogue instead of a monologue.)

   Like: "What do you like about your current situation?" (This builds trust and shows professionalism.)

   Alter: "If there was one area that you could alter, what would that be? (Listen for her response.) "Why does that frustrate you?" or "What specifically is the main frustration?" (This identifies her pain, and more importantly helps her realize she has a need.)

   Signer: "I don't want to step on anyone's toes, but if we were to take a look at a product or service that (insert what they want to alter), would this be something that you can move forward with today, or would we need to have other decision-makers involved in the process?" (This is a timesaving technique that qualifies her right off the bat.)

   Paint the Picture: "Let me make sure I'm hearing you right. What you have now is (insert what she said), and what you enjoy is (insert what she said), and what's frustrating is (insert what she said), and you said that if we were to take a look at a (insert your product or service) which helped (insert what she said she wanted to alter), then this is something you can move forward with today. Now, did I hear you right?"

After she says yes to this question, you will have a customer before you have even gone into your presentation!

3. You are creating a buying atmosphere. Again, people love to buy but they hate to be sold. So, when engaging in a selling situation, you need to let people off the hook and let them know it's okay if they don't buy. Try saying something like this: "What I'll do is show you how this works, and if you like it, that's great; if not, it's no big deal. It's not like I created/ invented (insert your product/service). The only favor that I ask is at the end of the presentation, just let me know one way or another. Does that sound fair?" Any time you sense your prospect's feeling of pressure is rising, use your buying atmosphere again and say, "As I said, if you like this, great; if not, it's no big deal. I just want to make sure you understand how this works."

4. You are answering some objections before they come up. For example: "If we were to take a look at a product or service that solved your need for (insert their need), then is this something that you can move forward with today? Or would we need anyone else involved in the decision-making process?"

Presentation

Many salespeople have the common misconception that the presentation should be the longest part of the cycle of the sale. In reality, the presentation should be the shortest part. There are a couple of universal objectives that you want to achieve in the presentation. The most obvious goal is to display the benefits of your product or service. Another objective of the presentation is to show that your product or service will meet the need—the "pain"—that was discovered in the introduction.

The presentation should be the shortest part.

Answering Objections

When it comes to answering objections, a couple of universal principles need to be applied. At The Southwestern Company, we follow the C.R.E.W. technique.

C—Calm them down by remaining calm and acting as though their objections are no big deal and are normal for them to be thinking. Relate to their situation. Use *feel, felt, found* as an effective way of relating to their situation. Say something like this "I understand how you feel. Actually John Smith felt exactly the same way. What he found was that after thinking through the details there were some solutions he didn't think about at first." Paul Schween says in his "Answering Objections" audio CD that you should have three renditions and variations of *feel, felt, found* to use based on the situation in which you find yourself. (For more information, go to www.ssnseminars.com.)

R—Re-sell the product or service you are offering. A good rule of thumb is to ask a question and then show another benefit of your product. So a master Navigator follows this rule: "Ask a question and then show another section." By asking questions that direct the conversation to help the prospect come to the realization that he does actually have a need for the product or service, the Navigator is sealing the deal.

E—Explain the situation. People don't care so much about what you think as they do about their own opinions. When explaining a purchasing situation to someone, it is always best to use his own words to get him to recommit to making the decision. A master Navigator will say something such as, "I remember you saying that this (insert product) is something your family needs. Also, you had mentioned that if we did take a look at something that meets your needs that you would want to go ahead and move forward with this. That is what you said, right?"

W—Work out a way. There are only four true objections: price, wrong time, not useful, or using someone else. There are hundreds of ways to work out a way for these four objections. If it's price, use a payment plan. If it's bad timing, then delay the payment. If they think they won't use your product or service, then re-sell your product by asking more questions and showing more "sections." If they are going with someone else, then explain your USP (unique selling proposition) and why they need to do business with you. *USP–The thing that makes your product or service different from anything else out on the market.*

Closing

The closing is often overlooked but is so important to the sales cycle. Without a proper close, there is no sale. You could have navigated the sales cycle and identified a problem, established a need, and presented a solution, but if you don't close the sale, nobody wins. The art of closing is all about navigating the pleasure or the fear of the buyer. Just as there are different ways to approach and present to the different buying behavior styles, there are different techniques to closing the different buying behavior styles. Fighters fear losing control, so you need to give them two positive choices. Entertainers fear rejection and not having fun, so you need to let them picture the fun they will have with your product or service. Detectives fear being wrong, so you should use logic to close the sale with them. Counselors fear change, so it's important to create a buying atmosphere. I'll get into the details of each closing behavior style later.

> *Fighters fear losing control.*
> *Entertainers fear rejection.*
> *Detectives fear being wrong.*
> *Counselors fear change.*

Regardless of which buying behavior you are closing there are universal success principles for closing.
- Have a standard close that you use word-for-word every single time.
- Lean back and relax during the close.
- Talk slow and low.
- Do not break eye contact.
- Close on minor points.
- Be assumptive and write up the order.

Referrals/Pre-Approach

Referrals are the lifeblood of the salesperson. It is essential to ask for referrals in order to have future prospects. By developing a referral-based clientele and applying the principles learned in *Navigate*, you will be able to connect with people and increase your business more than you can imagine.

Working a Navigate referral-based clientele is like adding turbo fuel to a Ferrari. You can plant seeds early on in the cycle by asking if they know of anyone who might have a similar need or who might be interested in your service or product. Take written notes and after the close, ask, "Based on who you are and who you know, who would be the person who could best benefit from using this (insert your product or service)? Maybe your neighbor, sibling, co-worker, or friend to offer them the opportunity to be a part of the program as well?" Then EXPECT to get referrals!

Pre-approach/Prospecting/Asking for Referrals

Pre-approach, prospecting, and asking for referrals is the foundation from which a rich book of business is developed. Pre-approach is also one of the best ways to identify someone's buying behavior style. Pre-approach is asking the right questions and doing your due diligence before ever engaging in initial contact. With pre-approach, the best time to gather this information is when asking for a referral—or you can simply use the everywhere-you-go approach.

A great example of how effective the everywhere-you-go approach can be was a time when I was selling in Anchorage, Alaska. It was my first day arriving in uncharted territory. I woke up early and proceeded to secure my soliciting permit at the county courthouse. While waiting for my permit, I struck up a conversation with the lady behind the counter. I asked her if she was familiar with The Southwestern Company and our products. She responded enthusiastically with a "yes." She had purchased the books five years before and enjoyed them. So I had her write a testimonial of how much she enjoyed the books.

What I used at this point in the story was a technique called *Planting Testimonials*. This easy technique will help your Navigate learning curve go a lot faster, and it will earn you a lot of money, too. When you run across people who already have your product or service, don't treat them as a waste of your time. Treat them as if they are gold! There are two main reasons why they are golden:

1. Referrals
2. Testimonials

How to Plant Testimonials*

1. Ask: "What do you like best about your product or service?"
2. Explain: "This really helps me describe the value of the product to potential clients, by using third-party testimonials. I really appreciate this!"
3. Plant: "If you could write down on this pad of paper what I heard you saying earlier about the value you received from the product and how much you've enjoyed it, ...!"
4. "Thank you so much!"

*Top producers have told me that this one technique alone is worth thousands of dollars—if you use it!

I continued mining the gold when I asked her a key question: "If you were I, selling books door-to-door, and you were looking for moms who were home early in the morning who would be interested in a product such as this; where would you start?" She pointed to a neighborhood on the map I had laid out in front of her. Then I asked another key question: "Based on who you are, who could I go speak with who would enjoy at least seeing great products such as those you already have?" She thought about it and was having a tough time thinking of an exact person, so I helped "JOG" her memory.

JOG is an acronym for a technique that will help you get referrals:

a.   **J**ust someone who might be interested (someone who could see the same benefit to our product as you do)—this creates a buying atmosphere;

b.   **O**nly people you know (co-workers, partners, friends, family, associations, church, sports teams, etc.)—this isolates faces and helps narrow their focus;

c.   **G**ive to get (I was talking with Mrs. Jones and she bought the product, then thought it was something that her sister two streets over should just take a look at to see if she was interested)—the more you give, the more you get.

—Zig Ziglar

After I helped her "JOG" her memory, she thought of a teacher who lived in that area. So then I went into pre-approach mode. I asked her the four important pre-approach questions:

1. What is the decision-maker's first name?
2. What is the best time to reach the decision-maker?
3. What is the decision-maker's cell phone number or the best number to reach her?
4. What kind of decision-maker is she?

Then I went straight to the teacher she recommended to me and sold her an eight hundred dollar set of books. Then I repeated the referral process and she gave me three referrals. Those referrals allowed me to sell another twenty five hundred dollars worth of books. I ended up helping eight families with their educational needs and collected over thirty five hundred dollars on my first day in the field.

While this sales cycle model has seven steps, I'm going to focus on the three steps that benefit the most from adapting your selling style to match the customer's buying behavior style: the approach, the presentation, and the close. It is important to make a connection within the first seven seconds of contact, which makes the approach one of the most important steps in the cycle, and presenting to the buyer successfully is essential to closing more effectively and efficiently.

Don't Believe the Lies

It was the fall after my first summer selling books for The Southwestern Company. I had been blessed by finishing as the number one first-year dealer in a field of more than twenty-five hundred salespeople, and I earned a substantial amount of income for a college student. Upon returning to the University of Tennessee for my junior year, I met a gentleman who found out how well I had done selling books. He started telling me lies about how I was doing way too much work with Southwestern and that I shouldn't have to work eighty hours a week to earn that kind of money. He supposedly had this grand scheme where I would receive $100,000 worth of on-line gift certificates if I invested $1,000 and found four other people who would invest $1,000 each, and I would be on the fast track to making millions in no time!

Well, I'm sure you can guess the result of this story. I actually took the bait and gave him the $1,000, but the worst part of the story is that I actually had one of my friends spend $1,000 on this get-rich-quick scheme that turned out to be nothing of value. Later we found out that the gift certificates were actually just pieces of paper with numbers on them with no real items available to be purchased. The lesson I learned through that experience is that there is no "secret" or "hidden key" to success. You can have the best idea in the world or be the best at navigating the sale but without forming the *habit* of putting in the work needed to succeed, nothing works!

Top-producing salespeople base their confidence in sales on work habits and acquired skills, not the result from a day, week, a month, or on natural abilities. They understand that the world of sales is simply a numbers game and applying the fundamentals with enough people is a formula for success.

Winners aren't always the most talented, but champions put in the most effort. Champions acquire the skills necessary to excel in their profession; they build their foundation of confidence on persistence and overcoming adversity. As Theodore Roosevelt said, "The credit belongs to the man who is actually in the arena, whose face is marred by dust and sweat and blood . . . who knows great enthusiasms, the great devotions; who spends himself in a worthy cause; who at the best knows in the end the triumph of high achievement, and . . . if he fails, at least fails while daring greatly, so that his place shall never be with those cold and timid souls who neither know victory nor defeat."

It is a natural tendency to look for the easiest route to success. Everyone wants the "get-rich-quick" formula. Rarely will you find a salesperson who will put in the effort and follow a system that has already been proven to work. One time I personally acted on the natural impulse to take the easy way to the big bucks—and that was all that I needed to learn my lesson.

The Foundation for Success

The foundation for success that I learned at Southwestern is made up of three basic elements: hard work, smart work, and coachability. After my second year of sales, I felt like I had worked as hard as possible, yet I didn't get the results that were my best. To reach my goal of breaking the company record the following year, I had to commit to becoming a true student of the game. Navigate is not designed to ask you to work any harder than you already are. But if you are like I was after my second year in sales—you don't feel that you can work any harder—the question you need to ask yourself is *Am I willing to work smarter?* If the answer is yes, then this system is for you.

> *The foundation for success that I learned at Southwestern is made up of three basic elements: hard work, smart work, and coachability.*

When it comes to being a student of the game, I am reminded of a time when I was in San Jose, California, at a ReMax real estate office. I was conducting an "Immediate Results" in-house customized sales training work-shop, and a gentleman in the corner was sitting with his arms folded and giving me a blank stare. I didn't think anything about it and went through my presentation. At the end of the training session, he stood up and addressed the group: "This training conference sounds great! I am going and I recommend all of you to attend." This gentlemen's name was Frank Liu who happened to be the sales manager of the number one ReMax office in the nation! So, as I like to do with all top producers I meet, I asked him, "What separates you from average producers?" His response was one that I will never forget. Frank profoundly stated, "Dustin, I live by this philosophy: *If you are not learning, then you are dying*." Mr. Liu was one of the oldest people on his team and yet he read new books, listened to new sales training CDs, and attended every training conference that was worth attending. Since he began living his life by this philosophy, and letting other great minds and ideas impact him, he has been at the top of his profession.

Top producers such as Frank Liu live by a philosophy of constant and never-ending improvement, and they follow selling systems they learn along the way, such as Navigate. This was the same philosophy I personally had adopted when I decided to become the top producer at Southwestern. I was determined to become a student of the game. Two things helped me build my confidence with setting my goal to be number one my first year with Southwestern. First was that other people had gone before me and proven that my goal could be accomplished. Second was that I had access to sales training, such as "Selling Like a Chameleon," advanced sales CDs, and sales talks from the other top producers who had gone before me. Let me ask you a question. Would you rather learn a tough lesson on your own through the school of hard knocks (pun intended) or would you rather learn from the mistakes of others? I chose the latter of the two and it paid off handsomely!

Sales is a numbers game!

I learned at an early age while selling M&M's for my little league football team that a good way to ensure success and a key to transforming into a little Navigate ninja was realizing that *sales is a numbers game*! Most of the guys on my team went out on one or two days and sold a couple of boxes of M&M's for our team fund-raiser. My grandfather Gene Caughron taught me two valuable lessons when helping me sell my M&M's: He told me we are going to knock on every door in our neighborhood, and some people will say yes and some will say no; either one is fine, but our goal is to at least see everyone. The second lesson he taught me was how to be assumptive; he taught me that when they come to the door, say, "Would you rather buy one bag or two?" and smile. If I had stopped after the first person told me no, I would have never learned how to work the numbers and feel the sensation of finishing successfully. The only guarantee is that **if you show more, you will sell more.** It's the "see more, sell more" philosophy. This also causes the *practice makes perfect* principle to come to life. As you go out and start practicing the principles taught in this book, remember the principles learned in this story: *See more and sell more, be assumptive, and practice makes perfect.* **The answer to every problem lies behind the next door!**

> *See more and sell more, be assumptive, and practice makes perfect.*
> *The answer to every problem lies behind the next door!*

Conclusion

To master the art of selling, it is important to first understand the sales cycle. While there are seven steps to the sales cycle, I'm going to focus on the three that are most affected by the Navigate method: the approach, the presentation, and the closing. Let's review four of the steps mentioned above.

What are the seven steps to the sales cycle?

1. PROSPECTING/PRE-APPROACH
2. APPROACH
3. QUALIFYING/INTRODUCTION
4. PRESENTATION
5. ANSWERING OBJECTIONS
6. CLOSING
7. REFERRALS

How does the pre-approach help you navigate the sale?
- LETS YOU IDENTIFY THEIR NAVIGATE BUYING BEHAVIOR STYLE
- HELPS YOU CONNECT AND BUILD INSTANT RAPPORT
- TELLS YOU WHO THE DECISION-MAKER IS
- SAVES TIME

What is most important about the approach?
- THE FIRST SEVEN SECONDS—YOU HAVE ONLY SEVEN SECONDS TO MAKE A GOOD FIRST IMPRESSION—TO MAKE A CONNECTION

What is a common misconception about the presentation?
- PEOPLE THINK IT SHOULD BE THE LONGEST STEP, WHEN IN REALITY IT SHOULD BE THE SHORTEST

What are the objectives of the presentation?
- TO DISPLAY THE BENEFITS OF YOUR PRODUCT OR SERVICE
- TO MEET THE NEEDS OF THE CLIENT

What is the art of the closing?
- NAVIGATING THE FEARS OF THE BUYER BY BEING AWARE OF THEIR FEARS TO HELP THEM MAKE A DECISION

For your free "Navigate Sales Diagnosis" go to:
http://www.ssnseminars.com/Sales-Coaching.aspx and click on the *chat live* button.

Also join our free e-zine at:
http://members.audiogenerator.com/info.asp?x=137686

PART TWO

The Compass

Chapter 3

The Four Buying Behavior Styles

The hardest person to figure out is yourself.

There is an art to selling. Some people refer to it as a game to be played or a dance to be gracefully two-stepped. As we discussed earlier, I like to think of the sales cycle as a body of water that needs to be navigated. With first-time customers, the salesperson is entering uncharted waters and must read the signs of the buyer in order to stay in the deep waters of the "sales channel," which is where the emotional connection is formed, trust is gained, and the sale is made. Selling someone something requires masterful communication. As my friend Tony Jeary says, "Life is a series of presentations," and becoming a master of Navigate will not only help you with your sales career, but it will also help you be a better communicator and influencer in life. Let's begin by examining the personality types and what makes people act the way they do.

No two people are exactly alike. Each individual is created differently. There are twenty-three chromosomes in the human body. These chromosomes come from both parents and can be in any various combinations. You could get your father's temperament but your mother's intelligence. Then throw into the mix the effects of conditioning and the type of environment in which you are raised, and the variations of human beings are endless. Because of this amazing degree of diversity, we see that everyone has a unique way of expressing feelings and emotions, especially when put into a high-pressured buying situation.

History of Personality

The great philosopher Hippocrates, considered the father of medicine, analyzed personal behavior types in the first century A.D. He came up with four very distinct behavior styles. "He based the four types on the predominance of certain bodily fluids: blood, yellow bile, black bile, and phlegm. That is how he named the types: sanguine (blood), choleric (yellow bile), melancholy (black bile), and phlegmatic."[1] While we now know that these fluids don't have anything to do with a person's personality, there is some consensus that the biochemical structure of the brain is related to a person's personality. Therefore, two people of the same personality type will most likely have the same biochemical makeup.

There are about as many personality analysis systems as there are people who administer them, such as counselors, employers, and sales managers. The DISC test, for example identifies the personalities as having Influence, Dominance, Compliance, or Steadiness. The Merrill-Reid Social Styles calls the four types Expressive, Driving, Analytical, and Amiable. The number one producing manager of the Countrywide/Bank of America mortgage division in America, Greg Goodman, trains his top-producing team with his own personality descriptions: the accountant, the salesman, the military soldier, and the counselor. Most people are a combination of two types of personality traits, meaning that there are two traits that are obviously more dominant than the others. *Strengths Finder 2.0* by Tom Rath is a great personality profile test that you can find at most bookstores or online at Amazon.com.

Personality profile tests are good for assessing a person's personality in general settings. For instance, knowing your personality type will help you in determining a career path, a role on a certain project, or even methods for working out struggles in a relationship. Buying behavior profiles, however, look specifically at how a person behaves in a buying situation. Similar personalities will behave differently in different buying situations—because money is involved. When someone is faced with the idea of parting with his or her money, the most timid person can become quite the fighter; the most artistic person can become very analytical. The reason for this is the phenomenon known as "loss aversion," which is the tendency for people to more strongly prefer avoiding losses than acquiring gains.

*Buying behavior profiles look specifically at how
a person behaves in a buying situation.*

According to a Yale University study, "This basic economic theory that people work harder to avoid losing money than they do to make money is shared by monkeys. . . . Tufted capuchin monkeys were given small disks to trade for rewards—apples, grapes, or gelatin cubes. The capuchins were asked to choose between spending a token on one visible piece of food that half the time gave a return of two pieces, or two pieces of visible food that half the time gave a return of only one piece. Economic theory predicts that consumers should not care which of these outcomes they receive since both are essentially 50–50 shots at one or two pieces of food. The capuchins, however, vastly preferred the first gamble, which is essentially a half chance at a bonus, rather than the second gamble, which is essentially a half chance at a loss."

It could be that our basic primal instinct is protection. As a mother bear instinctively does whatever is necessary to protect her cubs, we also do what it takes to protect our families, as well as our possessions. We would rather protect what we have than to risk it to try for gain. It makes sense on some levels and is seen as selfish on others. The Bible says that "the love of money is a root of all kinds of evil" (1 Timothy 6:10). It is good for us to not hold on too tightly to our material possessions, our money. Therefore, we do what we can to avoid any loss or even the perception of loss. This loss aversion can even mean changing our personalities and buying behaviors.

Buying behavior can be different even among similar personality types. Have you ever noticed that you behave a certain way when you're in a social situation, and sometimes a completely different way in a high-pressured selling situation? People behave differently in different situations. For instance, one analytical-amiable type person may approach buying as a fighter, wanting to know the value right away and to get to the point quickly. Another analytical-amiable person may be what I call the detective, wanting to see the charts and figures that support all the claims and to think through all the options. The second scenario is probably more common with analytical-amiable people, but it is not necessarily always the case, which is why understanding how to identify and adapt to the different buying behavior styles is so important in becoming a top producer. We all have buying behavior styles, and our own style is the way in which we tend to sell to others. Given the tendency to hold on to our money and avoid what we perceive as a loss, it is necessary to make an emotional connection with the buyer. The only way to make an emotional connection with the buyer is to sell in the way he or she wants to buy, so adapting your selling style is key.

Author's Profile

I learned a lot about myself when I took the Myers-Briggs and other personality tests. I learned that I'm a driver extrovert, which is the Myers' term for an outgoing team leader who is decisive and intense, as well as friendly and social. That means that I am a fighter/entertainer naturally, in a social setting. My buying style, though, is a little different. When I'm buying something, I tend to be an entertainer. I like to joke around with people and relish the conversation. When buying something, I want it to be fun and I want to be able to dream about what I can do with my new toy.

After taking The Navigate Profile Test, I realized my dominant buying behavior style was an entertainer. Upon realizing this about myself, I reflected back to my book of business and realized that almost all of my customers were of the same buying behavior style. I guessed it was because I was abiding by the Golden Rule: "Do unto others as you would have done unto you." Because I was really good at working referrals, all of my entertainer customers were sending me to their entertainer friends, and I had a nice book of business going. Once my mind was opened up to the Navigate principles of adapting to the four different buying behavior styles and following the philosophy of "do unto others as they would have done unto themselves"—in other words, communicate to people in a style in which they want to be communicated to—my production literally doubled!

"Do unto others as they would have done unto themselves."

Characteristics of Four Buying Behavior Styles

There are four distinct buying behavior styles and innumerable combinations of such styles. Just as people typically have a combination of two or three personality types, with one being dominant, people also generally have a combination of buying behavior styles, with one being dominant. It is important to be able to identify these styles early and adapt your selling style quickly.

The 4 buying behavior styles

- The *fighter* is a results-oriented buyer who needs action, is motivated by challenges, and fears losing control of the situation. Under pressure, the fighter lacks concern for others and can run over people.
- The *entertainer* is more people-oriented and expressive, is motivated by social recognition, and fears rejection. Under pressure, the entertainer is overwhelmed.
- The *detective* is a task-oriented perfectionist who is motivated by accuracy and fears making mistakes. Under pressure, the detective is overly critical of himself or herself, as well as others, and can seem negative.
- The *counselor* is a team-oriented listener who is motivated by maintaining consistency and is afraid of change. Counselors like guarantees. Under pressure, the counselor avoids controversy.

It is important to recognize the buying behavior in the first seven seconds in order to quickly make the emotional connection that will lead to success. We will discuss how to begin identifying buying behavior styles even before meeting face to face and how to identify the buying behavior style within the first several seconds of a face-to-face meeting, or on the phone.

Sometimes it can be tricky identifying the dominant style or the two most dominant styles. Once you are aware of the philosophies in this book, you will be able to adapt to all four buying behavior styles. Keep in mind, though, that not everyone is exactly the same and not every single characteristic and trait fits every person who might have a certain behavior style. As I describe in more detail the four buying behavior styles, I want you to identify which two you are the most like and which one you are the least like.

Fighter

Results-oriented and straight to the point, the fighters don't like to waste time on pleasantries. Fighters have an aggressive selling/buying style. A person with a fighter buying behavior style has little patience and is not afraid of conflict or rejection. They like challenges and will seem almost confrontational when trying to maintain control. *The main fear of a fighter is losing control.* The fighter needs to know what the benefits are, what the risks are, what makes this a good value for him or her. The question a fighter always will ask is **what.**

One time in my junior year of college, I had knocked on one of my last doors for the evening. I'll never forget the interaction that night. A lady opened the door and the first words out of her mouth were, "What are you selling?" She continued, "I don't care what you are selling and I don't have time to listen."

I followed up with a slight smile and said, "The reason I came by is because your good friend James Jones had nothing but great things to say about you. I promised him that I would at least swing by and show you what he and everyone else have been getting. I'm sorry it sounds like I'm in such a hurry, but I only have a few minutes to spend with each family. I know you're in a hurry just like me, so I'll just get down to the bottom line. I want to make sure you at least know what I'm doing."

She said, "You have two minutes. What are you doing?" Adapting to this obvious fighter, I went straight to my demonstration and she ended up buying from me.

Fighter

Traits: Results-oriented, Resilient, Determined to overcome odds

Fear: Loss of control

Under Stress: Runs people over

Key Phrases: "What do you want?" or "What is the price?"

Question: What?

Entertainer

Entertainers are energetic and outgoing people. When you meet an entertainer, be prepared to receive an earful because they love to talk. They want to build rapport and be your friend. Sometimes entertainers can be a little flashy or want to be impressive. Oftentimes entertainers are seen as having "the gift of gab." Some people consider them smooth talkers. Although they may be very talented, entertainers sometimes lack the discipline and organizational skills to maximize their gifts. *The main fear of an entertainer is rejection.* Entertainers want to know who knows about the product or service, who will be impressed, who else is buying the item. The question they always ask is **who**.

The first time I tried to sell to an entertainer was a memorable day. It was my first day selling books door-to-door, and I honestly had no idea what I was doing. The first person I ran into at 8:00 a.m. was a bona fide entertainer. She opened the door in her bathrobe and said, "Hello. Who are you?" I responded with, "Hi. How are you? My name is Dustin. I've been talking with all of the families in the area about the Southwestern study guides. I was just over at your neighbor Mary's, and I heard you were into your kid's education." She smiled, let me in, and bought.

Entertainer

Traits: Extroverted, Enthusiastic, Inspired by affirmation

Fear: Rejection

Under Stress: Overwhelmed

Key Phrases: "Hey, Buddy! How are you doing?" or "Who are you?" or "Who gave you my name?

Question: Who?

Detective

Detectives are very logical thinkers. They will always want the specifics and all the details you can provide. Don't be vague with a detective; you can count on them doing their homework and making a well-thought-out decision. The person with a detective buying behavior style is a perfectionist and a stickler for accuracy. Detectives need to have all the information before they make a decision. *The main fear of a detective is being wrong.* They ask why is this better than another, why do I need this, why should I buy it from you today. Their question is **why**.

Selling to detectives has always been hardest for me. I have to adapt the most when selling to detectives. Something funny happened when I first started teaching Navigate at our large Success Starts Now!™ (www.ssnseminars.com) sales training conferences all across the nation. After my first presentation, about 75 percent of my feedback forms were the best feedback a speaker can receive. The 25 percent of the feedback that was negative came from the detectives. They said things like, "You have no idea what we detectives are like." After watching the video of my presentation, I realized the irony of what I had done. My whole presentation was geared to the entertainers. I didn't have any statistics, percentages, or details backing all the years of research I've put into the Navigate system. They were not debating the content that was being delivered. They just weren't connecting with the way I was presenting Navigate! I found this to be very insightful, and funny, that Navigate not only applies to selling situations but also to presentations, normal everyday conversations, e-mail, and just about any form of communication.

Detective

Traits: Detail-oriented, Perfectionist, Motivated by accuracy

Fear: Making mistakes

Under Stress: Overly pessimistic

Key Phrases: "Why is this better than the other product?" or "Why is the price what it is?" or "Why will this improve my productivity?"

Question: Why?

Counselor

A counselor is known for being a team player. Counselors are often very family-oriented. They make slow decisions and are very methodical in their approach because they prefer the status quo and don't like to rock the boat. They prefer seeing the big picture and how what you are selling can help the group as a whole. A person with a counselor buying behavior style wants to make a cautious and wise decision. They are not risk takers. *The main fear of a counselor behavior style is change.* The question they tend to ask is ***how***.

A large commercial real estate firm engaged us in customized ongoing sales training. When I sat down with their CEO, I quickly perceived that he was a counselor. As soon as I had identified his counselor buying behavior style, I slowed down my rate of speech, leaned back in my chair, and said, "John, I know you and your team here at XYZ Commercial consistently provide quality work and that your clients know you are dependable. Before we dive into the details about seeing if there is a fit with helping train your team, I just wanted to assure you that we provide the same high quality and dependable service here at Success Starts Now!™, a division of the 150-year-old Southwestern Company. Our mission statement is 'We build people, and those people build great companies.'" Then he smiled, and we began our meeting.

Counselor

Traits: Team player, Active listener, Desires consistency

Fear: Change

Under Stress: Avoids controversy

Key Phrases: "How does this benefit the company as a whole?" or "How will this compare with what we currently are using?" or "How is this supposed to work?"

Question: How?

As you now know, people approach buying things with different perceptions, attitudes, and intentions. The best salespeople try to make a connection with the people to whom they are selling. They want to understand them and give them what they need. The top salespeople will quickly identify the person's buying behavior style and adapt his or her selling style to meet that need. The magic happens when you adapt to others. They will feel appreciated, valued, and respected and will be ready to adapt to you in turn.

Selling is transference of conviction. The way you make decisions is also the way you will expect your prospects to make decisions. A person's selling style is the same as buying behavior style. If you buy like a fighter, for instance, then you will naturally sell like a fighter. It is important that you understand your own buying behavior style, so that you will know when you need to adapt your selling style. If you know that you are a fighter and recognize that your prospect is a counselor, you know that you will need to adjust your style in order to make the connection more quickly.

> *Selling is transference of conviction. The way you make decisions is also the way you will expect your prospects to make decisions.*

Your Profile

As you read through the different buying behavior styles, did you consider which style you might be? It may depend on what type of buying situation you were imagining when reading the descriptions. Some people are more of a fighter when it comes to major purchases, such as a car, but will be more like an entertainer when it comes to more minor purchases, such as clothes. If you are the type of person who shops at three different grocery stores to get the best deal, you are probably a detective. If you analyze every detail of a car purchase but will buy the latest designer sweater because it looks so good, you may be a combination of a detective and entertainer. If you won't upgrade to a high-speed Internet connection, you may be a counselor who would rather maintain the status quo even if it means more inconvenience.

Are you a fighter, an entertainer, a detective, or a counselor? Consider the different buying behavior styles and determine where you fall. The more you understand the different styles, the better you will be able to put yourself in your customers' shoes and make a connection with them.

While there is a connection between personality styles and buying styles, it is not ever a hard-and-fast rule. Below is a chart that shows you which personality styles lean toward a certain buying style. Likewise, people with a certain buying style will have an easier time selling to people with the same buying style.

Personality Type Standard	DISC	Buying Style Sells Best to . . .	Personality Type Myers-Briggs	Buying Style Sells Best to . . .
Choleric	Dominance	Fighter	Expressive/ Introvert	Entertainer/ Counselor
Sanguine	Influence	Entertainer	Sensing/ Intuition	Entertainer/ Detective
Phlegmatic	Steadiness	Detective	Thinking/ Feeling	Detective/ Entertainer
Melancholy	Compliance	Counselor	Judging/ Perceiving	Fighter/ Counselor

In *Navigate*, we have identified the four main styles with which people make purchases: fighter, entertainer, detective, and counselor. You may already have an idea of what buying style you are. Below are four stories of a person buying a car. Each one illustrates a different buying behavior style. See which one you relate to most closely.

Jim Selling to Mark the Fighter

Jim was a good-natured salesman, one of the best on the floor. He had been with the dealership for more than ten years and was consistently one of the top producers. He was a well-trained Navigator and able to read the buyers and adapt his selling style quickly.

One day a gentleman named Mark came through the showroom door with a quick, energetic pace. He opened the door as though with a purpose in mind, pulling it wide. His pace was quick as he walked across the floor to where Jim was standing. Mark's arms were pumping as he almost hurried to greet Jim.

"I want to look at your midsize sedans," was the first thing Mark said when he reached Jim.

Being the Navigator that he was, Jim stood up and stuck out his hand firmly and said, "We can do that. I'm Jim. What's your name?"

The fighter buyer responded with, "My name is Mark, and I'm kind of in a hurry!"

Jim smiled and said, "Well, let's not waste any time. So you're looking for a midsized sedan. About what price range are you looking for: $25,000, or more like a fully loaded, cream of the crop $60,000 range?"

"I want the best bang for my buck."

Jim smiled back as he put on his coat and said, "Now, I want to make sure I know how to serve you best. Is this car just for you or is there anyone else involved with this decision? I wouldn't want to step on anyone's toes."

"It's just for me."

As they were walking out of the door and onto the lot, Jim said, "Great! So tell me, what are you driving now?"

"A Honda."

"What do you like about your Honda?"

"The gas mileage."

"Great! And what brings you here today? What's the main thing you are looking for in a new car?" Jim asked.

"My Honda is old, and I need something that will have little more pickup, and something that looks good," said Mark.

Jim said, "If we found something that is new, looks good, and gets good gas mileage, would that be something that you would want to jump on today?"

"Well, yeah," exclaimed Mark.

"I think we have a perfect fit for you."

Jim Selling to Amanda the Entertainer

The next day a lady wearing a bright orange dress and big hoop earrings energetically walked into the auto dealership. She bounced from car to car in the showroom and finally ended up at Jim's desk. She started with an enthusiastic, "Hello! How are you doing?"

Jim smiled as wide and excitedly as he could and replied, "Outstanding! How about yourself?"

"I would be doing much better if I had something dependable to drive!" exclaimed the lady.

"Well, lucky for you that's what I'm good at helping people find! What's your name?"

"Amanda."

"Well, hello, Amanda. I love your purple scarf. My wife has one that is similar that she got from New York. Where did you get yours?" She replied with a fifteen-minute monologue about the story of how she found her scarf. Then Jim continued, "So it sounds like you're excited about looking for a new car? What kind of car are you in now?"

She said, "I'm in a VW bug."

"Awesome!" exclaimed Jim. "What color?"

"Lime green."

"Cool. What do you like best about the VW? Why did you choose that one to begin with?"

Amanda replied, "I loved the color, and it's just cute!"

Jim said, "Okay, so what brings you in here today? I remember you saying that you're looking for something more dependable. I'm guessing that your VW is at the end of its rope."

"You got it!"

Jim said, "I think we've got something that you're going to absolutely love and look good in, but first I want to make sure I'm not stepping on anyone's toes. If we did take a look at a car that was dependable, fun, and cute enough for you to drive, would this be something that you want to move forward with today, or would we need anyone else here to take a look at the car with you?"

She smiled and said, "No, we're all good. It's just me."

Jim Selling to John the Detective

A reserved, neatly dressed man walked in one day. Jim noticed how perfectly pressed his khaki pants were and how methodical his steps were, with little movement from his arms. Jim stood up and stuck his hand out to introduce himself and said, "Hello."

The man quizzically looked back at Jim and shook his hand, then took two steps back and said, "Hi, I'm looking for a 2009 BMW 335i hardtop convertible with a sports package and alloy wheels."

Jim smiled and said, "Great! You strike me as a man who knows exactly what he wants. I appreciate it when guys do their homework on what they are looking for. Now, if I'm reading you right, it seems like you probably would like to know all of the details and options we have with all of our BMWs for a comparison. Am I right?"

The detective smugly smiled and said, "Sure."

Jim replied, "I'm sorry. My name is Jim. I didn't catch yours."

The man replied, "My name is John."

"Good to meet you, John. Do you mind if I jot down some specifics you are looking for in your BMW so I can identify whether we have one in stock or need to ship one from another location?" John didn't mind, so Jim proceeded to ask him twenty questions about what price range he was looking for, color, miles per gallon, etc. Then, Jim followed up with finding one on line that fit his exact specifications. He took John out to the lot and had him test drive a similar model while he explained all of the special benefits and details of the car he was driving. At the end of the day, John ended up liking the model that he drove better and loved Jim for taking the time to really find out what he was looking for.

Jim Selling to Beth the Counselor

One day a slow-moving, conservatively dressed woman strolled into the office. She slowly went from car to car in the showroom and acted as though she was just checking things out. Jim got up and approached the woman slowly. He walked up to the woman as she was looking at an Audi and said, "Did you know that the Audi is actually the only car that has a lifetime satisfaction guarantee?" (I actually made that up, but let's pretend Audi really did promote that.)

The lady shook her head interestedly and said, "No. How is that?"

Jim replied, "German cars have such a quality manufacturing process that Audi is actually that confident in their brand and work."

The counselor replied, "Well, that is interesting."

Jim said, "I'm sorry. My name is Jim."

As he slowly extended his hand and offered a sincere handshake, she replied, "My name is Beth."

Then Jim said, "Well, did you come in by yourself today or did you bring the family with you?"

Beth replied, "No. I left everyone at home."

"I see. You're just doing some reconnaissance? Or are you looking for something in particular?"

"Actually I'm looking for a new minivan," said Beth.

"We definitely can help you out with that," Jim replied. "But I don't want to step on anybody's toes. If we found the minivan of your dreams today, would you want to have anyone else here to take a look at it with you?"

Beth answered, "Yes, I would need my husband here for sure. We never make a decision without discussing it first."

"That's very wise," said Jim. "Let's do this as a professional courtesy to you and your husband. Let's find out when is the best time to get both of you here, and I guarantee we will find you the minivan that is safe, reliable, and dependable for the whole family. Is your husband available to come in now or would tomorrow be better?" Then Beth proceeded to set up an appointment with Jim and her husband for noon the next day, and they ended up purchasing a new minivan.

While reading the different scenarios, did you seem to relate to one of the buyers more than the others? With whom would you identify most closely: Mark the fighter, Amanda the entertainer, John the detective, or Beth the counselor? While these stories are exaggerated to highlight the verbal and nonverbal clues, they should help us to see how we tend to behave most like one of the styles when we are buying. To better identify your buying behavior style, take the behavior profile tests on the following pages. The first test, The Navigate Behavior Profile Test, should be taken quickly without thinking too much about your answers. It is designed to test you on an instinctual level, getting your initial response without a second thought. The second test, The Navigate Behavior Assessment Test, should be taken more slowly with more thought involved. It is designed to test you on an intellectual level, having you carefully think through each answer.

The Navigate Behavior Profile Test (Quick version)

There are ten groupings of descriptions below. While taking the test keep your mind focused on how you behave when buying or selling. For each group, rank the adjectives from 1 to 4, with 1 being most like you and 4 being least like you. When finished, total up each letter and write the totals at the bottom. See the next page for interpreting the test.

Assertive	2	A	2		Courageous	4	A	2
Optimistic	1	B	1		Extroverted	3	B	1
Detailed	4	C	4		Considerate	1	C	3
Neighborly	3	D	3		Supportive	2	D	4
Vocal	4	A	2		Adventurous	3	A	2
Engaging	3	B	1		Entertaining	4	B	1
Rational	1	C	4		Disciplined	1	C	4
Helpful	2	D	3		Pleasant	2	D	3
Competitive	3	A	2		Resilient	3	A	2
Social	2	B	1		Enthusiastic	1	B	1
Thorough	4	C	3		Prepared	4	C	3
Steady	1	D	4		Team Player	2	D	4

Aggressive	1	A	2
Inspiring	2	B	1
Cautious	4	C	4
Obliging	3	D	3

Energetic	1	A	1
Animated	4	B	2
Strategic	3	C	3
Thoughtful	2	D	4

Blunt	4	A	2
Influential	2	B	1
Modest	3	C	4
Friendly	1	D	3

Totals: A 25 B 22 C 23 D 18

Your largest number will indicate which style you are least like. The smallest number is the style you are. If you have a tie or near-tie, then you are a combination of styles.

A = fighter
*B = entertainer
C = detective
*D = counselor

Did this profile confirm or contradict your assumed buying style? Do you agree with the assessment?

The Navigate Behavior Assessment Test (Full version)

This test contains twenty-five groups of statements. It should take you about ten minutes to complete.

- Study all the descriptions in each group of four.
- Select the one description that you consider Most Like You when buying/selling.
- Study the remaining three choices in the same group.
- Select the one description you consider Least Like You when buying/selling.

For each group of four descriptions, you should have only one Most Like You and only one Least Like You.

Sometimes it may be difficult to decide which description to select. Please remember there are no right answers, so just make the best decision you can.

Remember—choose only one Most Like You and one Least Like You in a buying or selling situation.

C	I seek the advice of others.	? MOST	? LEAST
D	I am a very detailed type.	? MOST	? LEAST
E	I see myself as an outgoing person.	? MOST	? LEAST
F	I am very determined.	? MOST	? LEAST

Remember—choose only one Most Like You and one Least Like You in a buying or selling situation.

C	I tend to be rather timid.	? MOST	? LEAST
D	People tend to see me as a dependable person.	? MOST	? LEAST
E	I am good fun and have a lot of personality.	? MOST	? LEAST
F	I tend to be an aggressive type.	? MOST	? LEAST

Remember—choose only one Most Like You and one Least Like You in a buying or selling situation.

C	I don't like tempting fate.	? MOST	? LEAST
D	I am very helpful toward others.	? MOST	? LEAST
E	People like my company.	? MOST	? LEAST
F	I don't give up easily.	? MOST	? LEAST

Remember—choose only one Most Like You and one Least Like You in a buying or selling situation.

C	I tend to be a friendly person.	? MOST	? LEAST
D	I tend to be a cautious person.	? MOST	? LEAST
E	I am good at convincing people.	? MOST	? LEAST
F	I am a very determined person.	? MOST	? LEAST

Remember—choose only one Most Like You and one Least Like You in a buying or selling situation.

C	Loyalty is one of my strengths.	? MOST	? LEAST
D	I am obedient.	? MOST	? LEAST
E	I have a good deal of charm.	? MOST	? LEAST
F	I am always willing to have a go.	? MOST	? LEAST

Remember—choose only one Most Like You and one Least Like You in a buying or selling situation.

C	I don't like arguments.	? MOST	? LEAST
D	I am always keen to try new things.	? MOST	? LEAST
E	People describe me as high-spirited.	? MOST	? LEAST
F	I am always ready and willing.	? MOST	? LEAST

Remember—choose only one Most Like You and one Least Like You in a buying or selling situation.

C	I try to be obliging.	? MOST	? LEAST
D	I always take notice of what other people say.	? MOST	? LEAST
E	I am always cheerful.	? MOST	? LEAST
F	I have a great deal of willpower.	? MOST	? LEAST

Remember—choose only one Most Like You and one Least Like You in a buying or selling situation.

C	People say I am a sympathetic type.	? MOST	? LEAST
D	I have a tolerant attitude toward life.	? MOST	? LEAST
E	I am self-confident.	? MOST	? LEAST
F	I am an assertive person.	? MOST	? LEAST

C	I never lose my temper.	? MOST	? LEAST
D	I like things to be precise and correct.	? MOST	? LEAST
E	I enjoy having a laugh and a joke.	? MOST	? LEAST
F	I am very sure of myself.	? MOST	? LEAST

C	People see me as being generous.	? MOST	? LEAST
D	My behavior is well disciplined.	? MOST	? LEAST
E	I am always on the move.	? MOST	? LEAST
F	I persevere until I get what I want.	? MOST	? LEAST

C	I always consider others.	? MOST	? LEAST
D	I am an agreeable type.	? MOST	? LEAST
E	I do not treat life seriously.	? MOST	? LEAST
F	I enjoy competition.	? MOST	? LEAST

C	I tend to be a kind person.	? MOST	? LEAST
D	People can depend on me.	? MOST	? LEAST
E	I accept life as it comes.	? MOST	? LEAST
F	People say I have a strong personality.	? MOST	? LEAST

C	I tend to do what others want to do.	? MOST	? LEAST
D	I like things to be very neat and tidy.	? MOST	? LEAST
E	I enjoy having fun.	? MOST	? LEAST
F	People can't put me down.	? MOST	? LEAST

C	I am always willing to help.	? MOST	? LEAST
D	I respect my elders and those in authority.	? MOST	? LEAST
E	I believe things will go well.	? MOST	? LEAST
F	I get the job done no matter what.	? MOST	? LEAST

C	I am a rather shy person.	? MOST	? LEAST
D	I am always willing to follow orders.	? MOST	? LEAST
E	People find my company stimulating.	? MOST	? LEAST
F	I don't scare easily.	? MOST	? LEAST

C	I tend to be an easygoing type.	? MOST	? LEAST
D	I am not willing to change my opinion.	? MOST	? LEAST
E	I always look on the bright side of life.	? MOST	? LEAST
F	I like a good argument.	? MOST	? LEAST

C	I rarely raise my voice.	? MOST	? LEAST
D	I am very patient.	? MOST	? LEAST
E	I am a very social sort of person.	? MOST	? LEAST
F	I am a very self-sufficient sort of person.	? MOST	? LEAST

C	I tend to trust people.	? MOST	? LEAST
D	I like peace and quiet.	? MOST	? LEAST
E	I am very content with my life.	? MOST	? LEAST
F	I have a very positive attitude.	? MOST	? LEAST

Remember—choose only one Most Like You and one Least Like You in a buying or selling situation.

C	I tend to be very receptive to other people's ideas.	? MOST	? LEAST
D	I am a moderate rather than an extreme person.	? MOST	? LEAST
E	I am always polite and courteous.	? MOST	? LEAST
F	I enjoy taking a chance.	? MOST	? LEAST

Remember—choose only one Most Like You and one Least Like You in a buying or selling situation.

C	I tend to be a forgiving person.	? MOST	? LEAST
D	I am a sensitive person.	? MOST	? LEAST
E	I can mix with anybody.	? MOST	? LEAST
F	I have a lot of energy and vigor.	? MOST	? LEAST

Remember—choose only one Most Like You and one Least Like You in a buying or selling situation.

C	I control my emotions.	? MOST	? LEAST
D	I am very conventional in my outlook.	? MOST	? LEAST
E	I enjoy chatting with people.	? MOST	? LEAST
F	I make decisions quickly.	? MOST	? LEAST

Remember—choose only one Most Like You and one Least Like You in a buying or selling situation.

C	I tend to keep my feelings to myself.	? MOST	? LEAST
D	Accuracy is very important to me.	? MOST	? LEAST
E	I am very friendly.	? MOST	? LEAST
F	I like to speak my mind.	? MOST	? LEAST

Remember—choose only one Most Like You and one Least Like You in a buying or selling situation.

C	I feel satisfied with life.	? MOST	? LEAST
D	I like to handle things with diplomacy.	? MOST	? LEAST
E	Most people find me accessible.	? MOST	? LEAST
F	I am very daring.	? MOST	? LEAST

Remember—choose only one Most Like You and one Least Like You in a buying or selling situation.

C	I am always ready to help others.	? MOST	? LEAST
D	I like to behave correctly.	? MOST	? LEAST
E	I have a very wide circle of friends.	? MOST	? LEAST
F	I find it difficult to relax.	? MOST	? LEAST

Remember—choose only one Most Like You and one Least Like You in a buying or selling situation.

C	I am a very calm person.	? MOST	? LEAST
D	I am a neat and orderly person.	? MOST	? LEAST
E	I am very active, both at work and at play.	? MOST	? LEAST
F	I generally get my own way.	? MOST	? LEAST

Tally up all of your Fs, Es, Ds, and Cs. Figure out all of your Most Likes and all of your Least Likes.

F = fighter
E = entertainer
D = detective
C = counselor

F		E		D		C	
+	−	+	−	+	−	+	−

Write the Most Like here:_____

Write the Least Like here:_____

*For your FREE one-on-one personal consulting "Navigate Sales Diagnosis" go to: http://www.ssnseminars.com/Sales-Coaching.aspx.

Conclusion

Were you at all surprised by the results of the tests? Do you agree with the results? For some of us, our behavior styles are more obvious than others. For some of us, we didn't need the tests but could figure out our behavior styles just from the illustrations. For others, it's not so clear and the tests help us to understand how we buy and, thus, how we sell. The most common result of these tests is not to identify our main styles but to see how close we may be to a combination of styles, such as a fighter-detective or a counselor-entertainer (it's not common, but it can happen). When you are a combination of styles, when your secondary style is almost as strong as the primary style, it means that on some days when in a certain mood that secondary style may be more dominant. It's important to know what tendencies you have when selling in order to be most flexible. If you are a fighter-detective, with your detective style almost as strong as your fighter style, and you are feeling under the weather or have just finished crunching some numbers (think "left brain"), you may sell more like a detective that day. When a fighter sells to a counselor, she will have a hard time suppressing the high energy and quick reasoning urges. The detective will be able to slow down more easily and take the time the counselor will need to make a decision.

Knowing your buying style means you know your selling style. Knowing your selling style equips you to be able to adapt quickly. Adapting to the prospect's buying style is essential to making a connection quickly and effectively. Let's review:

Fighter—results-oriented, needs action, motivated by challenges, fears losing control, asks what.

Entertainer—people-oriented, expressive, motivated by social recognition, fears social rejection, asks who.

Detective—task-oriented, perfectionist, motivated by accuracy, fears making mistakes, asks why.

Counselor—team-oriented, listener, motivated by consistency, fears change, asks how.

For your free "Navigate Sales Diagnosis" go to:
http://www.ssnseminars.com/Sales-Coaching.aspx and click on the *chat live* button.

Also join our free e-zine at:
http://members.audiogenerator.com/info.asp?x=137686

Chapter 4

Identifying Buying Behavior Style

Awareness is the key to reading someone.

Identifying the Four Buying Behavior Styles

Communication is defined in academia as the act of conveying information from one person to another. There always has been communication. It's just that the means of communication have changed over the centuries. In antiquity, when people wanted to convey a message—to get a point across, to teach a lesson, to remember their history—they told stories. Societies, centuries ago, were based on oral communications. That may be why when people think of communication today, they tend to think of the conversations we have with each other. What comes to mind when you think of communication? Do you think of television or radio news or sportscasts that give us information? Or do you think of the written word? If you are from an earlier generation, you might think of newspapers, magazines, and books. Today's generation most likely thinks of Web sites, blogs, and text messages. A recent study reported that the top six ways of communicating for people under the age of thirty are:

1. Text messaging
2. Instant messaging
3. Social networking (MySpace, Facebook, etc.)
4. Face-to-face
5. Phone
6. E-mail

These are most certainly forms of communication, but if this is all you think of, you are only scratching the surface. In the study of communication, you will find that we transfer messages to one another in two main ways: verbal and nonverbal. The former is the most direct way because it involves words, but it is also the most unreliable method because we all tend to put on a good face. (More about face reading later.) For instance, when you have taken someone through your entire cycle of the sale, at the end he may say that he's interested in your product or service. However, when you follow up with him the next week, then a week later, and you never get through to him or hear back from him—I know that has never happened to you before—you now know what he was really doing was saying whatever would get rid of you. Another example is when you sit down with someone to go through your pricing structure and as soon as you tell her your price, she crosses her arms and scowls. When you ask if the price is within her budget, she says "yes," but she then comes up with some other excuse to procrastinate on making a decision. Likewise, a gentleman might see his boss at a meeting, avoid eye contact with her, and fold his arms tightly across his chest before offering a short, "Good morning." What he really means is, "I can't believe you gave me that impossible deadline. I hate my job. I'm upset with you right now and wish you would go jump in a lake." These niceties are just our way of being polite. Remember when your mother told you that if you can't say anything nice, don't say anything at all? It is good for society that people don't always say what they think. Because of this tendency, however, hearing the words is not the best way to understand what people are really saying. Verbal communication, the words we use to convey our message, accounts for only 15 percent of the message. Nonverbal communication, which constitutes the remaining 85 percent of the message, is made up of various means of communicating—from the tone of our voices to the way in which we shake hands. Therefore, you must learn to "hear" or read the nonverbal forms of communication to know what people are really saying. Because the verbal form of communication is not the main way of transferring a message, I won't be focusing as much on verbal communication here. While there are hundreds of forms of nonverbal communication, for the sake of space I'm going to focus on seven and categorize them as Pre-approach—identifiers you can recognize before a face-to-face meeting—and Approach—identifiers that you can observe in person.

> *Verbal communication, the words we use to convey our message, accounts for only 15 percent of the message. Nonverbal communication constitutes the remaining 85 percent.*

Verbal Clues

Verbal communication, while the most direct and obvious form of communication, is not always the most reliable. People don't always say what they mean, they may not have the right words, or they may just be flat-out deceptive. Whatever the case, it's important to be able to look for key words or phrases when identifying—or to confirm—a person's buying behavior style. (Many times you will have identified a person's style before you ever hear a word uttered from his or her lips.) It is also important to identify the volume in a person's voice, whether it is a low or high volume, and whether it is a fast or slow speed.

Fighters are results-oriented. They don't want to waste time on pleasantries. Their sentences tend to be short and choppy. To confirm that you are talking to a fighter, look for phrases or questions such as "What do you want?" or "Just tell me how much it is."

The **entertainer** is the one who loves to talk. Entertainers are social people who fear rejection. Part of their defense mechanism is to talk continually so they don't have to risk hearing a negative comment about themselves. They may start the conversation with a story about some celebrity gossip or sporting event to break the ice. They will say a lot of things. However, to confirm that you are indeed speaking to an entertainer, look for phrases such as "Hey, Buddy! How are you doing?" or "Who are you?" or "Who gave you my name?"

Detectives are logical thinkers. They are perfectionists who need all the details before making a decision. Their sentences tend to be short and choppy. Detectives tend to ask: "Why is this better than the other product?" "Why is the price what it is?" "Why are you calling?"

The **counselor** is family-oriented and a team player. Counselors don't do well with change. It will take longer to sell to a counselor than to the other buying behavior styles. Counselors, unlike entertainers, are not talkative; they tend to be laid-back and more introverted with their communication. They will ask questions about how something will impact the team or how it will improve communication and camaraderie. To confirm that you are talking to a counselor, look for phrases such as "How does this benefit the company as a whole?" or "How will this compare with what we currently are using?" or "How is this supposed to work?"

Verbal clues are by nature clues that are received during your initial meeting, when you are talking to the person. It is very rare that you will be able to get verbal clues at the pre-approach stage. Below are some of the most common types of verbal clues that help you identify a person's buying style.

Responses

Not only do top producers listen for what voice quadrant someone is speaking from (which we will discus later), but they also listen to the actual words being said. When identifying buying behavior styles, you want to listen for the main question that each style naturally asks.

Fighters: What?	Entertainers: Who?
Detectives: Why?	Counselors: How?

The Navigational Opening Question

When cold-calling or just calling someone you have never met before, have a prepared ice-breaker to cut the tension of a sales call, and also to help you identify the buying behavior style of the person you are calling. Our team at Success Starts Now!™ (www.ssnseminars.com) is trained to have a written script with the following line on a note card and to keep it next to the phone so we remember to say: "Hi. Is this (insert first name)? (Pause and wait as if you are asking a question.) This is (say your first name and last name), and if you are trying to put a face with my name it probably won't work because we haven't met yet." (Pause and wait for a response.)

This type of greeting is very effective for determining the buying style of the person on the other end of the line. It's not meant to be suave or slick and it may even irritate some, for example, fighters. The point is just to identify the style. You can adjust your selling style once you find out what type of person you are dealing with. Here is what you are looking for.

Fighters will answer the phone with a loud and direct tone and an authoritative slow and controlled speed in their voices. Fighters will typically start out with an authoritative "Hello." After you go through the Navigational Opening Question, they will probably say something like, "Okay! What can I do for you?" Fighters will typically not be amused by your engaging opening statement, so they might pause for a while and then respond with a serious, "Okay." Don't panic when a fighter responds this way. Later in this book we will talk about how to adapt to the different buying behavior styles once we have identified them. Our goal is simply to identify our prospect's buying style ASAP. Listen for their *what* questions.

Entertainers will answer the phone with a loud upbeat tone and a fast and excited speed. After your Navigational Opening Question, an entertainer may ask for your name again and say something like "Who is this? Oh, Dustin! Hey! How are you doing today?" Entertainers will find humor in the opening statement and you might hear a slight chuckle in the background. Listen for their *who* questions.

Detectives will answer the phone with a low quizzical tone and a fast and calculated speed. Detectives won't sound as irritated as a fighter, but will probably come back with something like, "Okay, why are you calling?" Detectives are similar to fighters with not much of a sense of humor when receiving a statement like this. Again, it's okay if they don't respond with arms wide open; we are listening for their *why* questions.

Counselors will answer the phone very softly and slowly. A counselor will be the person who picks up the phone and gives you a soft, barely audible mumble of a hello. They will reply with a welcoming, "How may I help you?" Counselors might not even respond to this statement at all. If you hear just silence on the other end of the call, you might be talking to a counselor. Listen for their *how* questions.

Voice inflection

Inflection is the final verbal clue indicator of a person's buying style. This is where the voice will change volume—typically from low to high. According to Dummies.com, inflection is the wave-like movement of highs and lows in the pitch of your voice. The peaks and valleys in your voice let your customers know how interested (or uninterested) you are in what they're saying. Inflection also reflects how interested you are in what you're saying to the customer. When inflection is missing, your voice can sound monotonic (read: boring and tedious).

Tone of voice

A third way of identifying a person's buying style before meeting face-to-face is by reading the tone of his or her voice. The tone of voice is probably the best way of identifying over the phone someone that you have never met before. If your job entails cold-calling on the phone, I would suggest tearing off the Navigate reminder page (which is similar to the chart below) at the end of this book and putting it next to your phone to remind you of how to identify the four behavior styles and how to adapt to the way they want to buy. Entertainers and fighters are usually more animated in tone. They tend to show their emotions more than counselors and detectives, who are less tonal. Counselors desire not to rock the boat or draw attention to themselves, so their tone is more subdued. Detectives think more about the details and tend to use their voices just to convey information rather than as a performance.

This is a voice quadrant diagram created by my business partner, Rory Vaden. He originally designed this to help teach how to evoke emotion when delivering a speech. We are using the same principles to identify buying behavior styles.

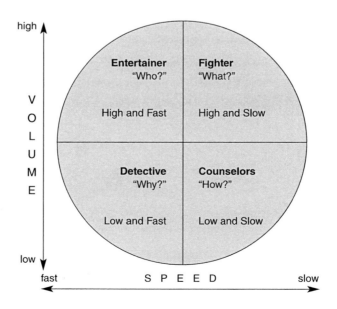

Nonverbal Clues

There are a number of nonverbal forms of communication, everything from the tone or inflection of a person's voice or facial expressions to the way someone walks or shakes hands. The way people dress or decorate their offices can even give valuable information about who they are and how they buy. I'm going to focus on seven of the primary nonverbal forms of communicating. Most of these are clues that you can pick up on only after the approach. There are three, however, that you sometimes can observe during the pre-approach. These are outlined below.

Pre-approach

The pre-approach is the step at which you gather information before initiating contact with someone. Sometimes you will have the opportunity to do some research on someone before meeting them in person. There are numerous ways to access information on a potential client. The pre-approach has gotten so much easier with today's technology and the ability to identify buying behavior styles by evaluating the language of text messages, use of emoticons, and someone's signature on his or her e-mail. So much information is readily available at your fingertips with tools such as Google and other search engines, social networking sites like FaceBook and LinkedIn, and archived business articles. You can always research companies or individuals by looking on their Web sites. And, of course, there are always the traditional methods of gathering information, such as by asking other people.

There is something magical about having information beforehand and being prepared for each sales call that can help you make the sale go more smoothly. To use the pre-approach as a tool to navigate your approach to different behavior types, simply ask the question, "What kind of decision-makers are they?" Based on the answer, you will be able to determine what behavior style they are, and have some "silver bullets" to use when approaching the different behavior types! If you have such opportunities, than you have three means of identifying a person's buying behavior style even before even meeting on the phone. If not, as we just discussed there are a few other main ways to identify buying behavior during the pre-approach: tone and inflection of voice on their answering machine and the way the person responds to your questions on an email.

There is something magical about having information beforehand and being prepared for each sales call that can help you make the sale go more smoothly.

Occupation

A person's occupation will reveal a lot about him or her. Most occupations require a certain behavior style in order to properly execute the daily functions of the job. There is certainly an association between someone's personality and his or her occupation and, likewise, there is an association between one's personality and his or her buying behavior style. People with dominant, aggressive personalities gravitate towards occupations that require grit, stamina, and physicality, such as law enforcement or the military. People who are reserved and focused tend to take up occupations that are less physical, such as professors or technicians. As we already discussed, detectives can always be found as CPA's, accountants, or engineers. If you think about it logically, wouldn't it make since that these jobs all require someone who is detail-oriented and somewhat of a perfectionist?

If you are in a sales role or you're a sales manager, then probably a majority of the people that you deal with on a day-in and day-out basis are either fighters or entertainers. Statistics show that 65 percent of all salespeople are either fighters or entertainers (and usually mixed with another style, as well). The world of sales can be a tough one—it involves hard work; putting yourself out there and communicating with people every day; and being persuasive enough for someone to buy from you. Both fighters and entertainers are extroverted and persuasive, which is what is needed to excel in the world of sales.

Counselors typically find themselves in support roles. They typically are not the frontline talent that is out closing a deal. Counselors make great managers or administration staff. I find a lot of high-level CEOs have developed counselor characteristics. Because the decisions that they make affect so many people, they need to make sure that everyone is on the same page and no one is going to be rubbed the wrong way. Typically, you won't find a CEO of a large corporation jumping to a decision without seeking counsel first.

Fighters will typically be found in your harder B-2-B type sales environments, such as printing and commercial real estate. Also, you will find fighters in the quick transition sales, such as auto dealers, mortgage bankers, and stockbrokers.

Entertainers can be found in the more relational-type sales jobs, such as real estate, financial advising, advertising, pharmaceuticals, or retail.

Below is a chart highlighting some basic occupations and the buying behavior styles to which they lean. This chart is a generalization and is meant only to give you a broad picture. There most certainly are exceptions to these classifications.

Occupation	Characteristic	Buying Behavior Style
Doctor	People-oriented and/or results-oriented	Entertainer and/or Fighter
Lawyer	Results-oriented and/or detail-oriented	Fighter and/or Detective
Professor	People-oriented and/or detail-oriented	Entertainer and/or Detective
Technician	Task-oriented and/or team-oriented	Detective and/or Counselor
Scientist	Task-oriented and/or team-oriented	Detective and/or Counselor
Businessman	Results-oriented and/or people-oriented	Fighter and/or Entertainer
Restaurateur	Results-oriented and/or people-oriented	Fighter and/or Entertainer
Warehouse	Task-oriented and/or results-oriented	Detective and/or Fighter
Military	Results-oriented and/or team-oriented	Fighter and/or Counselor
Police Officer	Results-oriented and/or team-oriented	Fighter and/or Counselor
Salesperson	People-oriented and/or results-oriented	Entertainer and/or Fighter

This chart is just a 10,000-foot look at a general overview of buying/selling behavior styles based on occupation. I have met plenty of stellar sales professionals who were detectives and counselors.

Office décor

Sometimes you may have the opportunity to visit someone's office or home for a face to face meeting and you can identify their buying behavior style before ever having to say a word. If such is the case, a person's office reveals a lot about his or her personality and thus buying style, so long as the person has the freedom to decorate as he or she wishes.

Fighter—An office with a wall showcasing awards, degrees, and certificates indicates that she is motivated by recognition and is probably someone who defines herself by her achievements. This person is most likely a fighter.

Counselor—The person who shows off the drawings of a three-year-old and displays family photos or pictures of their team at work reveals a person likely to be a counselor, or one who greatly values their family or team.

Detectives—A neat and tidy office is usually the sign of a detective. I always enjoy messing around with detectives. Once I've identified a detective and I am walking into his office, I'll take a piece of paper and set it down on his desk cock-eyed. Then I'll take a step back and count to see how long it takes him to straighten up the messy piece of paper.

Entertainers—A messy office will typically belong to an entertainer. A lot of entertainers organize their offices by the P.I.P. system (Post-it Planning). The funny thing about an entertainer's office is that when you question her about how messy her office looks, she will reply in a confused fashion and will probably tell you that it is clean, with everything exactly where she wants it.

Handwriting

If you get the opportunity to look at a person's handwriting or signature before meeting him or her, see if it's small and neat, small and messy, large and neat, or large and messy. Typically, entertainers will write **in large, somewhat messy lettering**. They don't pay attention to the ideas and words so much as how they appear. The fighter will usually write *more messily than neatly*, but the lettering won't be so large because he isn't as concerned with a flamboyant appearance. Counselors tend to write *in messy smaller letters*, while detectives typically write *in small neat handwriting*.

The "Counselor's" office with family pictures displayed

My "Entertainer" office in Nashville, Tennessee

Approach

Body language

Body language can give you more of an insight into someone's mind far beyond the words that he chooses to say.

Fighters have body language that resembles a drill sergeant in the military. When they walk into a room, it's as if they are on a mission, like Arnold Schwarzenegger in *Terminator*. They pump their arms up and down and walk in a direct path to where they are going. Many times they are a little tenser than the average Joe and they seem to always be on point, or at attention. If you are sitting at a desk or board table with someone who takes both hands and puts them together, forming a steeple with his fingers, he or she probably has some fighter tendencies.

According to the study of body language, when you position your hands in the "steepling" manner, it represents the need for control. So, if we observe someone has the need for control, we are going to deduce that he or she is probably a fighter.

Entertainers have body language that resembles a bouncy ball. Imagine a politician pinball that bounces from one point to the next, happily waving and shaking hands along the way. If you notice someone cannot sit still, is always acting fidgety, and seems to have Attention Deficit Disorder (ADD), you might be speaking with someone who has an entertainer buying behavior style. When sitting at a desk or in board meetings, look for the person who talks with his or her hands and you have found the entertainer in the group.

Detectives have body language that resembles a judge in the courtroom, like Judge Judy, with a very skeptical look on their faces. If you have the feeling that someone is skeptical and not naturally trusting, you might be talking to a detective. When sitting at a desk or in board meetings, look for the person who is poised and sitting upright and proper, perhaps taking calculated notes or making calculations on a calculator, and you have found the detective in the group.

"Steepling"   *"Talking With Hands"*

Counselors have body language that resembles a slow-moving bus. Imagine a slow-moving bus, making many stops, making sure everyone is on board. Counselors care more about others than they do themselves, so their body language is usually very open and is receptive to what you have to say. If you notice that you've been in a group of people who all have been sharing ideas and philosophies, and there is someone who has been observing and not trying to throw in his or her two cents' worth, you might have a counselor on your hands. Counselors typically will observe for a while and then provide an educated response that is insightful and considerate of everyone's opinions.

*"Open End Receptive
Body Language"*

Face reading

The art of face reading is an ancient practice. It was originated by the Chinese over a thousand years ago. The Chinese called it *mein sung*, which translates into "reading faces." The emperor used to have mein sung face readers at the entrance to his palace to read the faces of anyone who entered, and thus to know what type of persons they were from the lines of their faces. In his book *The Amazing Face Reader*, Mac Fulfer says **"A face can be read like a map that points the way to a deeper understanding of yourself and of every person you meet."**

Since studying, I've noticed some colorations to people's buying and selling behavior styles based on the lines of their faces! Here is what my research has shown.

When reading faces, you want to look for the most predominant feature or line on an individual's face. This is a general overview of what my research has found. I am not trying to say that if you see these lines on someone's face, that person is 100 percent a certain buying behavior style. But what I am saying is that more times than not, this is a good clue of where that person spends his or her time in thought.

"Fighter Freight Train Focus Line"

Fighter

Fighters possess two distinct facial features: One is the "freight train focus line." Whenever you see someone who is thinking about something and a deep line forms between his eyes, it comes from intense focus on a task at hand over a lifetime. When you see this line, it should cue you that he is focused on the task that is on his mind and you should just to cut straight to the point! The second is a notch in the middle of the nose. If you see someone with a noticeable hump on his nose, it means that when backed into a corner, he will more likely "fight" than "flee." So, in a high-pressure situation, he is ready for the gloves to come out.

Entertainer

Entertainers' faces are fairly easy to read. For starters, you can just look at the shape of their oval or round-shaped heads, which is your first clue that you have a fire-filled, enthusiastic extroverted entertainer. The next place to direct your eyes is to the entertainer's full, round meaty, cheeks. Having meaty cheeks indicates that someone can maintain high levels of energy for an extended amount of time. Also, it means that someone has spent an extraordinary amount of time smiling and laughing. Due to all that laughing and smiling, the entertainers develop a line we call the laugh line.

So, the next time you are at a business mixer and someone bops over to you who has a round head and full cheeks with deep laugh lines showing, you will start to build more rapport and talk about people that you know that she also might know. Make sure to give her a sincere compliment about her wonderful smile.

"Entertainer Smile Lines"

Detective

Detectives are detail people. Think about the CPAs, accountants, or engineers you may know. Do you notice some similarities in their facial features? Let's think about this logically; all detectives are somewhat perfectionists and are very calculating in their thinking. The main fear of a detective is being wrong. Because of that, a lot of detectives can be described as pessimistic, or, as they would call themselves, "realists."

"Detective Eyes"

A common characteristic of detectives is to have narrow features, such as an upside-down triangle or a diamond-shaped head. Also, detectives tend to have a recessed chin and/or a narrower nose. A thin, long nose indicates that one is financially conservative and thrifty with his spending.

Look for the lines on the face of the detective and see which direction the lines on the corners of her eyes and mouth are facing. If the lines are slanted down, then you are probably talking to a pessimistic "realist." And lastly, take a look at the ears of your potential detective. For the most part, detectives have smaller ears, which means that they are not risk takers (which fits right in with the detective's biggest fear—being wrong).

Counselor

According to mein sung, counselors have the natural element of water in their face. Counselors' features are very loose and almost flow with their faces. One of the most predominant features to look for on a counselor is a large, broad-based nose, which indicates the counselor is a giver and wants to make sure everyone is happy. The next thing to look for is low-set ears.

Low-set ears indicate that someone is a slower decision-maker and doesn't make quick, impulsive decisions.

"Counselor Nose And Ears"

Counselors want consistency and strongly desire to make everyone on the team feel loved and part of the common goal. Due to never-ending selflessness, a counselor's face changes with his mindset. I've known people who in their youth were a fighter selling style and had a narrow nose with high-set ears.

Then they were put into a management role, or started their own business, and after having to focus on building a team and making good practical business decisions, their faces morphed into counselors with low set-ears and a wide-based nose.

Your face will adjust to the focus of your mind.

"Fighter Ears"   *"Counselor Ears"*

Walking Style/Handshake

You can tell a lot about a person just by the way he walks and by shaking his hand. Some people say that you can tell whether or not you can trust someone by the way he shakes your hand. The tradition of shaking hands is a cultural ritual. So when identifying buying behavior styles based on someone's handshake, make sure he is from a culture where shaking hands as a form of greeting is normal.

Fighters will approach you as if on a mission. Remember the body language of the drill sergeant? Guess what . . . they walk the same way. They pump their arms up and down and walk with a fast pace. When they extend an arm to shake your hand, their hand in a jabbing motion like a knight's sword thrust, they will typically have a rigid thumb, indicating authority. When you shake their hand, they will do one of two things, if not both. One, they will apply more pressure than is normal. Two, they will turn their hand on top of your hand. Both of these characteristics indicate a need to assert control. Remember, the fighter's fear is loss of control!

"Fighter Handshake"

Entertainers will approach you much like a movie star walking on a red carpet or a politician leaving the stage after a motivational speech. They usually are smiling ear to ear with their fiery faces glowing. Their arm movement typically is a carefree swaying motion. They might be waving at you ahead of being within earshot. They usually will approach and give you a warm, loving greeting. When they shake your hand, they are not scared to overextend themselves or to get out of the normal sphere of comfort. They might be inclined to give you a hug, maybe a pounding of the knuckles, or perhaps even a high five! They typically will come in for a handshake with a submissive position, having their hand already on the bottom with palm turned up, wanting to show an open, friendly greeting. They just want to be friends. Remember that the entertainer's biggest fear is rejection!

Detectives will stroll from one point to another, carefully observing every person and everything they come into contact with. They might walk up to you as if they are wondering why they are even talking to you. They typically keep their body under control and try not to reveal anything about themselves. Detectives will often walk with no motion in their arms and will take short, calculated steps. When a detective reaches out to greet you, he is hyper-sensitive of his sphere of comfort, so he will very calculatedly approach you and barely extend his hand to greet you. Then, after engaging in a short, soft handshake, he will immediately step back into his comfort zone. Remember, a detective's fear is being wrong!

Counselors will walk into a room with a carefree manner and flow to their walk. A lot of counselors are pocket people. They love the security and comfort of having their hands in their pockets as they walk. Counselor typically will analyze the situation and might offer a warm and caring handshake, or they might just keep to themselves and leave their hands in their pockets, giving you a head nod, turning the other way, or ignoring your handshake move. Realtors usually can relate to the head-nod-turn-the-other-way-ignore-your-handshake-move from running into counselors at open houses. Remember, the reason a

counselor might not shake your hand is that his biggest fear is change.

"Counselor Hesitation Handshake"

Dress

You can tell a lot about someone's buying behavior style by the way he or she dresses. Everything we do consciously as we put ourselves together in the mornings is a reflection of our subconscious—not to mention that the clothes, accessories, hairstyle, and shoes are all things that we have chosen to purchase already.

Don't try to fit people into a certain category just because one day they wore a certain type of shirt. This is merely a general overview of common ways the four buying behavior styles dress.

Fighters wear solid colors and solid patterns. For example, a male fighter in business attire would probably be wearing a power suit and a power tie, and he will probably have his shoes shined, indicating he is ready for business. If you ever see a man wearing a solid red tie, he probably has some fighter in him. Fighters tend to be attracted to the colors red and black. A lot of fighters will wear all black all the time. Remember, fighters' biggest fear is loss of control, so they dress in an authoritative manner. Donald Trump is a good example of how a fighter would dress.

Entertainers will wear bright colors with fun patterns in their clothing. They also are the buying behavior style that will want to dress to impress. Look for fancy jewelry, expensive watches, wedding rings you can ice-skate on, big loopy ear rings, etc. For example, a female entertainer in business attire would probably be wearing a brightly colored shirt under a coat with big shiny buttons, and she might wear a chunky gold necklace that matches the three golden rings on her hands. An excellent example of an entertainer is Julia Roberts at the Academy Awards.

"Entertainers"

Remember that the entertainer's biggest fear is rejection. When they put themselves together, they want to be accepted and they dress to impress.

Detectives are perfectionists. Imagine how a perfectionist would dress, and you will have a pretty clear picture of how a detective dresses. Typically, they will wear a neutral-colored, modest outfit, probably with the shirt tucked in and the pants pressed. Back in the days of pocket protectors, detectives would enjoy the organization

"Detectives"

and convenience they provided. Remember that a detective's biggest fear is being wrong, so when he gets dressed, you can count on nothing being out of place.

Counselors like consistency. Do you know someone who wears the same thing almost every day? Or has a comfortable style that is not very different from day to day, rather like Inspector Gadget? Counselors typically dress for comfort and aren't very concerned with what other people think about how they dress. They are more focused on other people than they are on themselves. Remember that a counselor's biggest fear is change, so if he is wearing an outfit from back in the nineties, he probably has some counselor in his buying behavior style.

"Counselor"

Conclusion

While you now know the characteristics of the buying behavior styles and should be thinking about or have an idea about what your own buying style is, in the next chapter I will go into more detail determining your buying behavior style. Once you determine your style, you will better know to whom it will be easier for you to sell and for whom you will need to adjust your style to make a connection.

What are the four different buying behavior styles?
- FIGHTER
- ENTERTAINER
- DETECTIVE
- COUNSELOR

What are ways to identify the buying styles?
- WORDS
- TONE OF VOICE
- FACIAL EXPRESSIONS
- OFFICE DÉCOR
- HANDSHAKE
- DRESS

With what kinds of people do you find it easiest to connect?
With what kinds of people do you have a challenge connecting?
How can you improve your sales?

For your free "Navigate Sales Diagnosis" go to:
http://www.ssnseminars.com/Sales-Coaching.aspx and click on the *chat live* button.
Also join our free e-zine at:
http://members.audiogenerator.com/info.asp?x=137686

PART THREE

The Journey

Chapter 5

Navigate the Approach

The Rule of Seven
You have seven seconds to make a first impression, and that impression will stay with them the next seven times you meet!

The approach is the spearhead of the sales cycle. If you don't plan your approach carefully, you are setting yourself up for failure.

The approach can involve research, gathering the background information about a prospect. It can also involve being on point and paying attention as you are approaching a new prospect. You can sell to people without knowing anything about them, but it is harder because it requires you to navigate more quickly the unknown. It requires you to be more skillful, gathering and processing information as you talk. If you are able to do your homework ahead of time and identify the person's needs and the buying behavior style before contacting him or her, you will be able to maximize the Rule of Seven.

When to Adapt Your Selling Style

What is the Rule of Seven and what does it have to do with making a first impression? The Rule of Seven says that we have only seven seconds to form a first impression with somebody. So what does that mean? That means that in that small window of time people will make judgments based on everything from your handshake and eye contact to your appearance and verbiage. The first seven seconds are a key to making the sale! Everything from your hair to your shoes, from your walking style to your eye contact, can be the difference between success and failure during the approach. The words we say within the first seven seconds are another huge factor. If we say anything other than something that appeals to them, we could potentially lose the sale!

When I began selling books door-to-door, I was treating each person as if they were all the same type of buyers. What I came to find out was that if I changed my words just a little bit, enough to match their buying style, within the first seven seconds of contacting them, my success rate doubled. I would connect with them and get in the door twice as many times as before. It caused my business to literally double from one year to the next.

Testimony

A great and vivid example that happened to me last year was when I had set up a first meeting with a prospect and his Managing Director. It was Monday morning; the meeting was set for 9 a.m. I arrived and Peter greeted me in the usual way, offering coffee, water, or tea. He proceeded to walk me to his company boardroom, where he said, "Lars, I did not think you would mind, but we hold our Board meetings the first Monday of every month and knowing how hard it is to get hold of all the decision makers I thought you would relish the opportunity to present to them all. You are first on the agenda, and they will all be here in 10 minutes . . . is that okay?" Of course, I said that was fine, but I did have to challenge my self-talk initially! To keep this example brief, they all arrived and funnily enough, the MD, your classic Fighter, took control straight away and would have run the presentation if he could have. The Finance Director, a Detective, was really listening and taking notes, but I could see he was pretty skeptical about how effective sales training was. The Sales Director, an Entertainer, was almost too vocal and was creating a selling atmosphere instead of a buying atmosphere. The Personnel Director, the Counselor, was doing his best to keep the conversation calm, but was being very noncommittal. Thanks to having been trained in Navigate by The Southwestern Company and dealing with different personality styles at the same time, I allowed the MD to get his objectives for possible training out in the open quickly. I invited the Finance Director to share his skepticisms and had the Personnel Director help deal with them openly. I gave the case studies and testimonial letters to the Sales Director and the Personnel Director, as they need and like Third Person Validation; gave the training and module options to the MD and Sales Director, so that they could choose options; and gave the Finance Director information on how we track activity and use it to help improve performance accurately. An hour later, after having said very little, but just questioned and listened to the Board debate their opinions, the MD wrapped up by saying, "Well, I guess you can see we could really use your help . . . What do you think?" I told them that I felt I had taken up enough of their time and would get back with a summary of their situation and some recommendations. Two weeks later that company became a client.

Lars Tewes
Founder of SBR CONSULTING

Learning the different approach techniques—learning how to navigate your behavior style during the first seven seconds—is crucial. It's the difference between being a mere producer and being a top producer. In the following pages, I give you some tangible verbiage to use in the approach, the first seven seconds—whether you're talking on the phone or if you're talking in person—to adapt your selling style (which is your own buying style) to the four different buying behavior styles *during those seven seconds*.

Approaching Fighters

Fighters will begin a conversation, whether on the phone or in person, in one of several different ways. They usually will use the word "what" within seven seconds. Or they'll answer the phone in a more abrupt, aggressive way, even to the point of saying "What do you want?" A fighter's voice will be louder than the voices of the other behavior styles. Whenever I find myself talking to a fighter, I know that I'm going to have to adapt my selling style. By nature my selling style is more cordial. I want to begin the conversation on a personal level and say, "Hey, how are you doing today?" Instead, I bite my tongue and get right to the point: "The reason that I called is . . ." Fighters want you to get right to the point. Remember, fighters are results-oriented and need action. So when selling to fighters, I make sure I tell them in the first seven seconds why I'm calling. If I meet them in person, I give them a firm handshake and say, "Is it (insert their first name)? The reason I came by is . . ." or if I'm on the phone, I say, "The reason that I called is . . ." These words resonate with fighters. You're speaking their language, and they're thinking, *"Great. You're getting to the bottom line. Let me hear what you've got."*

Role Play

Wrong: Richard Approaching as an Entertainer

Richard calls a fighter and says, "Hello, Mr. Jones! How are you?"

The fighter replies, "What do you want?"

Richard says, "My name is Richard and I'm with XYZ Company. I wanted to call and ask you a couple of questions."

John Jones says, "Sorry, I'm not interested." Then he hangs up.

Right: Richard Adapts His Style

Richard calls the fighter and says, "Hi, John?"

John replies hesitantly, "Yes . . ."

Richard continues, "My name is Richard Sales, and if you're trying to put a face with a name, it probably won't work because we haven't met yet."

John replies, "Okay . . ."

Richard keeps going. "The reason I'm calling is that your company came up as the top insurance company in Nashville, and what I'm doing is talking with all of the top producing salespeople in the area, making sure they are aware of the big conference coming to town on February 20th called 'What Separates Top Producers from Average Producers.' Have you heard about it yet?"

John replies, "No, but tell me more."

Fighters require less rapport, so don't beat around the bush. Richard is an entertainer. The first scenario shows how frustrating it can be for fighters to be approached in a friendly manner with niceties when all they want is for you to give them the gist—get to the point. Give them value statements quickly, and be clear and specific on how your product or service is going to impact their bottom line. Don't ever argue with fighters. They are convicted people who know how to win arguments. If they disagree with you, try to find out more information. Ask why? They like to be in control, so ask for their help. Be sure to give them a lot of choices and challenge them in a positive way. Answer their *what* questions as you noticed in the second scenario, where Richard adapted his selling style and answered the *what* questions right away.

Approaching Entertainers

My buying behavior style is that of an entertainer. Therefore, I sell most naturally as an entertainer. The way I naturally want to begin a conversation, whether on the phone or in person, is with some pleasantries. The first thing I want to say during those first seven seconds is, "How are you doing today? I was just speaking with (insert a name that they recognize), and I have heard nothing but great things about you." That is how an entertainer wants to be approached, so I don't have to adapt my style to approach an entertainer. However, if you are a fighter, counselor, or detective, you will need to adapt your style to build more rapport, and drop some familiar names.

Role Play

Right: Richard Approaching as an Entertainer

"Hello! Is it Samantha? How are you today?"

"Great! How are you today?"

"Excellent! I was just speaking with our good friend Kimberly, and she had nothing but great things to say about you. Did I catch you at a good time?"

Wrong: Amy Not Adapting Her Fighter Style

"Hi, Samantha. This is Amy from XYZ Company, and I am calling to see if you would be interested in lowering your mortgage payment by 10 percent?"

"No." Click.

As you can see in the first example above, Richard the entertainer matched Samantha's entertainer style well. Richard began by building rapport and by dropping names of some people they know in common. **Dropping power names or dropping names that entertainers recognize answers their number one question: *who.*** They're thinking, "Who are you and who do you know that I know?" so if you drop names on entertainers within the first seven seconds, that will connect with them and they will like you and trust you because of the connection they have with the person that you know. They think, *"I know and trust that person; therefore, I like and trust you."* If you drop names on them after building rapport, after asking how they're doing, if you can do it within the first seven seconds, the first impression that they'll have of you will be a good one, and you'll find yourself making a sale that you might not have otherwise as happened in the second scenario. Samantha didn't want all the details right away. She wanted to get to know Amy first, to build rapport.

Approaching Detectives

Details are important to detectives. They are task-oriented and are motivated by accuracy. You'll want to say the word *detail* and provide them with some numbers and percentages within the first seven seconds. That will get their attention and let them know that you are speaking their language. You should give them numbers and percentages. For example, give them a time frame of how long the conversation's going to last. That will usually allow you to make a connection in the first seven seconds. Think of an accountant you might know or an engineer. Imagine the following exchange taking place between a salesperson and your friend or associate.

Role Play

Wrong: Richard Approaching as an Entertainer

"Hey, Andy! How are you doing today, brother?"

"Okay."

"Great! Hey, I've got a great deal that's the best thing you've ever seen ever! You are going to love this! It's exactly what you've been dreaming of!"

Andy coldly responds, "I'm not interested." Click.

Right: Richard Adapts His Style to a Detective

"Hi, Andy?"

"Hello."

"Yeah, this is Richard, and I'm calling to update you on that project we were talking about last month. It's 20 percent less than the last figure I showed you. Do you have five minutes?"

"Yes. Five minutes, sure."

Now, would the second scenario be a pretty good initial contact to that accountant or engineer you know? It should be, because in the second instance Richard was speaking the detective's language. He connected with Andy, and Andy will meet with Richard and possibly buy from him just because of that seven-second introduction. However, notice how in the first example the exchange was awkward, choppy, and forced at the beginning. It was hard to get through the first seven seconds and it didn't leave a favorable impression. Andy ended up hanging up on Richard after that exchange.

Approaching Counselors

With the counselor, again, you want to use choice words. The words you want to use with them are "team" and, if they don't have a team, talk about their "family." So if you're selling real estate, talk about how this is a neighborhood that's going to help their family and it's going to be consistent and growing. Those are all good words: *consistency, team* or f*amily*, and *growth*. The real hook with counselors, however, is the word **guarantee.** If you can guarantee something, that's music to their ears. It can be something as easy as, "I guarantee you're going to really like doing business with me," but, of course, you will need to follow through. Whenever they hear that word, I guarantee you, it gets their attention and causes them to like you and trust you. When selling large ongoing sales training packages to counselors who run companies across the nation, I make sure to mention how our training is based on 150 years' worth of proven sales strategies and principles that have been tried and are true. Let's see how it doesn't and does work in the following exchanges.

Role Play

Wrong: Richard Approaching as an Entertainer

"Hi, Lisa. How are you doing today?"

"I'm fine."

"Great! The reason I'm calling is to see if you would be interested in living the life of your dreams with one of our newly renovated time shares?"

Lisa responds abruptly, "No."

Right: Richard Adapts His Style

"Hi, is it Lisa?"

"Yes."

"My name is Richard, and I know we haven't met yet but our good friend Rory Vaden passed your name on to me. He had nothing but great things to say about you. Rory was telling me that you were one of his most trusted friends, and he guaranteed me that it would be worth my time to contact you and let you know how I can help your team the same way I helped his. Did Rory give you the heads-up that I would be giving you a call?"

Lisa responds, "No, but he is known for not doing such things. How may I help you?"

Notice that in the first exchange Richard was being too emotional and "salesy" right off the bat and tried to see a grand vision. Counselors are good listeners who are afraid of change. The extroverted style Richard used in the first scenario came on too strong and exuded action and change. Counselors need to take things more slowly. They don't like pressure to make quick decisions but need to run things by the team or someone that they know. When Richard adapted his style in the second scenario, Lisa was much more receptive to him and willing to hear him out. It will take some time and effort to sell to a counselor, but when you do make the connection it will be a long-term relationship with long-term yields.

> *The key to adapting your approach is to change what you are doing. Don't give in to fear. Just go for it!*

Factors to Reach Maximum Navigate Potential

The reason people do not try techniques such as Navigate and, therefore, do not reach their true potential is because they build barriers—belief barriers—that cause self-doubt. As John C. Maxwell describes in his book, *The 21 Irrefutable Laws of Leadership*, people naturally create belief-restricting "lids." Most people don't believe they can hit high goals.

The three most important characteristics for breaking belief barriers are commitment, control, and confidence.

1. Commitment is doing the work—putting in the effort with no excuses! Top producers do not make excuses; they stay committed.

2. Top producers focus on the things in life that they can control, such as the number of hours to work, the number of calls to make, the attitude to have. They focus on what I call R.A.F.T.

   R—They Realize that an event is occurring.

   A—Accept the situation.

   F— Focus on the controllable.

   T—Transform the negative into a positive.

3. Confidence is a key factor in being a top producer. People are attracted to unconditional confidence. It evokes trust, and people will be led to take action when around someone with such confidence.

For more information on techniques such as R.A.F.T. and philosophies such as unconditional confidence, check out my previous book, *Speaking of Success*, at www.ssnseminars.com.

Adapting to the Different Buying Styles

Adapting to Fighters

Do . . .

- Give value statements quickly.
- Be clear and specific about the reason you are calling on them.
- Challenge them in a positive way.
- Answer their *what* questions.

Don't . . .

- Begin with pleasantries.
- Try to build rapport.
- Beat around the bush.

Adapting to Entertainers

Do . . .

- Begin with pleasantries.
- Build rapport.
- Be enthusiastic and energetic; complimenting and encouraging.
- Drop names of people they know.
- Answer their *who* questions.

Don't . . .

- Come on too strong at first.
- Push to the presentation too quickly.

Adapting to Detectives

Do . . .

- Be prepared to give details.
- Match their controlled tone of voice.
- Answer their *why* questions.

Don't . . .

- Spend a lot of time talking about yourself.
- Offer your opinion.
- Be vague about expectations or fail to follow through.

Adapting to Counselors

Do . . .

- Take it slower with them.
- Tone it down and speak in a casual, personal manner.
- Answer their *how* questions.

Don't . . .

- Come on too strong.
- Pressure them to make a quick decision.
- Allow them to be the only one in the room with you.

Conclusion

As we discussed, the key is to use the techniques learned in the Navigate system within the first seven seconds. It takes discipline, it takes practice, and, more than anything, it takes awareness. You have to be aware of the four different behavior styles and be looking for them. Then, when you see that you're talking to one of the different behavior styles, you have to adapt. You have to use some of those tangible techniques that we were just discussing, and I promise you'll see a big difference in your productivity, communication skills, and in your relationships if you navigate to their behavior styles.

As a review, here is some verbiage to use with the four behavior styles within the first seven seconds:

Fighter

"The reason I'm calling is . . ."

It's important to get right to the point with the fighters. This answers their *what* question.

Entertainer

"How are you doing? John, head of marketing, gave me your number."

Entertainers desire rapport and want to feel like you care about them. The second part of this technique is dropping a name that they recognize. This answers their *who* question. Using a name they recognize causes the prospect to associate you with the friend they like and trust.

Detective

"I can save you 50 percent in the first three months of your plan."

These are your accountant-types. They want details, numbers, percentages, and time frames. By giving them details early, you are addressing their *why* questions.

Counselor

"I guarantee this five-year plan will promote consistent growth and teamwork." Use your name brand if it's well-established.

These things answer the counselors' *how* questions.

For your free "Navigate Sales Diagnosis" go to:

http://www.ssnseminars.com/Sales-Coaching.aspx and click on the *chat live* button.

Also join our free e-zine at:

http://members.audiogenerator.com/info.asp?x=137686

Chapter 6

Navigate the Presentation

It's not the best presenter who wins; it's the one who presents the most who wins.

The presentation is the step of the sales cycle in which you show off your product or service. It is when you present to the buyer all the features and benefits of your product or service. You must establish that yours is the best out there for the price and that it will satisfy the needs of the buyer, will solve a problem, and make his or her life better. If you have done your homework, conducted your research ahead of time, and found out exactly who you are dealing with; if you have approached the buyer with confidence, adapting his or her buying style; if you have built good rapport with a qualified buyer, the presentation need not be a long affair. Rather, it should be the shortest step in the cycle. If you skip all the preliminary steps in the sales cycle and jump right to the presentation before they trust you, before you know their needs, the presentation will take a long time because you will not only be giving them information about your product or service, but you will be trying to build rapport with them at the same time. We call this "throwing mud on the wall" and hoping something sticks.

The presentation should be the shortest step in the cycle.

When to Adapt Your Selling Style

When you have had a chance to do some homework and know the type of person to whom you are going to be presenting, you can make adjustments to your presentation ahead of time. (Now that you know the four different buying behavior styles, I recommend you prepare four different presentations. Practice them and be ready to adapt your presentation on the fly.) If you didn't have the luxury of knowing who you are selling to before your approach, you definitely should know the buyer's behavior style by the time you present your product or service. You certainly don't want to bore an entertainer with details or instill doubts in a detective by describing elaborate pictures of them using your products.

Presenting to Fighters

As we've seen so far, fighters are action-oriented. They want you to get straight to the point. Don't waste their time with a lot of preliminaries when it comes to the presentation. If you have built good rapport and established yourself well by showing that you mean business and that you're there to show to them quickly that your service will solve their problem, you shouldn't need to spend much time on the particulars. By now, they should know that you won't waste their time and should be willing to hear you out. Take less time reporting all the statistics. Instead, get to the bottom line of what helps them, and use key action words. They want to hear things like "the reason this will help you" or "the options you have here are" or "the bottom line is." Remember, fighters are afraid of losing control. In your presentation, give them options. Sell them on only a couple of selling points and then go to the close.

Role Play

Wrong: Richard Presenting as a Detective

"Well, Josh, let me show you all the features of this car that I enjoy the most." Richard proceeds to point out a dozen or so features, taking ten minutes. What Josh hears is, "Blah, blah, blah, blah, blah."

Josh then says, "Okay, I'm late for a meeting. I've got to run. Thanks!"

Right: Richard Adapts His Style

Richard says, "I remember you saying the main thing you want is bang for your buck. Well, check this out. Compared to anything else in the market, this lasts longer, gets better gas mileage, looks better, and gives you more bang for your buck. Pretty cool, huh?"

Josh then says, "Yes, it looks good."

Notice how frustrated Josh became when Richard used a detective style to present to Josh. He didn't want to hear about all the features of the car that Richard thought were so cool. Josh felt as though his time was being wasted, when all he wanted was to get to the bottom line right away: What is this going to do for me? What is this going to cost me? What is my return on investment? The main question of fighters is *what*, and the sooner you can answer those questions the better. When Richard adapted his selling style, the presentation took no time at all, just as it should. He got right to the point and answered all Josh's objections before he could even raise them.

Presenting to Entertainers

The key to presenting to entertainers is to keep it fun! Entertainers are people-oriented and like to interact. You will probably spend a lot of time building rapport with entertainers, and, quite possibly, almost as much time presenting to them. As I said above, the presentation shouldn't be a long affair. It should be the shortest part of the sales cycle. However, with entertainers it may take a little longer than with fighters, because entertainers are relational and like talking to people. If done properly, though, the presentation to entertainers can be short and sweet. They react better to a presentation that paints a picture, that tells a story. Dream with them. Paint a picture for them of their future. Let them see themselves enjoying the benefits of your product or service. Ask them, "What benefit would you see yourself enjoying the most about this product/service? Is it the _____, _____, or _____?" If you're selling a car, emphasize the sex appeal, speed, or cool new GPS and stereo system. Use bullet points with entertainers to keep their attention.

Here is an example of the right and wrong way of selling a house to an entertainer.

Role Play

Right: Richard Presenting as an Entertainer

"Samantha, if I'm reading you right, it seems that you're the type of person who enjoys having a good time. One of the best features of this location is that it is two blocks away from the most vibrant part of town. Just imagine being able to walk to everywhere you want to go! Also, what's great is that with a little elbow grease, this house is a great fixer-upper investment and five years down the road you should be happy with its appreciation in value."

Wrong: Amy Not Adapting Her Counselor Selling Style

"Well, this house seems to be all right. I know the roof isn't that good. And the gutters need to be repaired. What do you think?"

Entertainers react to a presentation that paints a picture. Richard was able to give Samantha what she needed, a vision of herself using the house five years from then. She was able to dream about her problems melting away and imagine herself having fun and purchasing a good investment. If you are using a powerpoint with an entertainer buyer use interactive videos that are funny to illustrate your point.

Presenting to Detectives

Details, details, details. Detectives are all about the facts and figures. They need to know the nuances of the service or the intricacies of the product. Your presentation to a detective will probably be as long as to an entertainer. It won't be as short as to a fighter, but with the proper preparation and by having all your data handy, it shouldn't be a long step. Have all your materials handy. Provide all of the details. Show graphs and charts. Cover every possible objection. Bring up the common objections for them and then shoot them down. Done properly, you can go through these quickly. Just remember: don't sell with emotions; sell with facts.

Role Play

Wrong: Richard Presenting as a Fighter

"Andy, can you see that this is something that you need? This price is for today and today only, so I recommend you go ahead and buy this bad boy."

Right: Richard Adapts His Style

"Here are the graphs, figures, and charts all on this PowerPoint. It includes a comparative analysis of the competition for you to review. Can you see how logical a decision this can be?"

As perfectionists, detectives need to have all the facts so that they can overcome their fear of making a mistake, or missing some vital piece of information. As you can see in the first example above, Andy was desperate for all the details, but Richard was more interested in pushing Andy to make a decision. Andy didn't let his emotions get the better of him and was actually annoyed at those tactics when all he wanted was to know: Why do I need this product? Why is this product better? Why will this save me money? Detectives need to know the answer to their *why* questions. In the second scenario, Richard adapted his style and got right to the details, answering all of Andy's why questions before they came up. That shortened the presentation time and allowed Richard to go right to the close.

Presenting to Counselors

Because counselors are not risk takers and generally make slow decisions, the presentation to counselors usually takes longer than to the other buying behavior styles. That doesn't mean that you need to be there all day. It just means that you need a little more patience with a counselor than you would with, say, a fighter. If you have done your homework, are prepared, and adapt your style, it should be a pretty quick process. When presenting to counselors, you will need to focus on the big picture of how your product or service affects the whole team. You need to show how the purchase will provide stability in the long run, will bring everyone together, and will make a stronger team. Focusing on these aspects of what you have to offer will help you be able to move to the close that much faster.

Role Play

Wrong: Richard Presenting as an Entertainer

"As you can see, this is the most awesome product ever! Can you see how much fun using this is going to be? My favorite parts of this are the bright colors and the cool body style. You are going to love this!"

Right: Richard Adapts His Style

"So what I'm going to do is show you a couple of these properties, and like I said before, if you like them, great, but if not, it's no big deal. I'll still be your friend, whatever you decide. I was meeting with John the other day, and he was telling me the main thing he looks for in a house is finding a location where his children can get a great education. Now, based on what you were telling me earlier, that was a main focus of yours. Was that right? These two houses in this neighborhood seem to be right up your alley, and I guarantee you that the schools in this district will help provide your kids with the education you are expecting. I think the main reason everyone feels secure about choosing our real estate company to work with is because of the 150 years' worth of experience we have in developing a superior full service realty company. Southwestern is one of the most dependable companies in America."

What did Richard do wrong when he tried to sell as an entertainer? He didn't focus on the long-term stability that a counselor desires. It's important when presenting to a counselor to be organized and focus on the stability and benefits to the team. In the first scenario, Richard pitched the product in a purely emotional way. This will not give you the connection you need with a counselor. When Richard adapted his style to sell as a counselor, he could more easily make a connection. He emphasized the stability of the company and the value of the service that the company will render. He was able to see that she needed a reliable house and dependable company. When that became the angle of his pitch, he was able to move quickly to the close.

Three Types of Confidence

When trying new techniques such as navigating their presentation, people will naturally go through different levels of confidence. There are three types of confidence: false, conditional, and unconditional.

1. **False confidence** is saying you can do something, but deep down inside you think there is no way you can actually do the task. It is negative self-talk. When someone talks and acts as though he is a super salesman but when put into an unfamiliar selling situation changes from superman to super-scared, he exhibits false confidence. False confidence comes from F.E.A.R, which is defined by Tony Robbins as *False Evidence Appearing Real*.

2. **Conditional confidence** is when you get your confidence from your last presentation. It is much like being on a roller coaster. If someone has a great day of selling, she is confident. If someone has a poor day of selling, than she loses her confidence. This confidence is conditional on the outcome.

3. **Unconditional confidence** is what you should be striving for. It is the type of confidence that is common to all top producers. It is based on knowing that you do have the necessary skills. Your self-worth is based on your effort and not on your most recent performance.

A person with unconditional confidence doesn't expect success all the time and can still be fearless in the moment. He knows that failure is temporary and success happens with perseverance.

Adapting to Fighters

Do . . .

- Be clear and specific about how your product is going to impact their bottom line.
- Challenge them in a positive way.
- Answer their *what* questions.

Don't . . .

- Be vague about particulars.
- Give them big picture ideas.
- Beat around the bush.

Adapting to Entertainers

Do . . .

- Be enthusiastic and encouraging.
- Sell the big picture with lots of sizzle.
- Ask their opinion and dream with them.
- Keep things fun by using stories and testimonials.
- Provide bullet point brochure to help with retention.
- Answer their *who* questions.

Don't . . .

- Bore them with details.
- Give them too many facts and figures.

Adapting to Detectives

Do . . .

- Provide a lot of details.
- Use charts, graphs, and figures.
- Be specific and remain objective and not overly emotional.
- Answer their *why* questions.

Don't . . .

- Give big picture generalizations.
- Force a quick decision. Allow them time to go over and analyze the details.
- Fail to follow through.

Adapting to Counselors

Do . . .

- Make sure they understand product benefits.
- Ask for their opinion.
- Be supportive and take charge gradually.
- Discuss how the team will benefit.
- Answer their *how* questions.

Don't . . .

- Be demanding.
- Force quick decisions.

Conclusion

You have seen the different ways to approach different people. Some need a more friendly, warmhearted approach to get them going. Some need a more down-to-brass-tacks approach to make a connection. Likewise, the presentation, as you have just read, will need to be adjusted and adapted to match the different buying behavior styles. Some people want more facts and details, while others want the big picture, a story behind the product or service. If the proper approach is made and rapport is built, the presentation should be the shortest step in the sales cycle. To recap the best presentation methods for each buying behavior style, here is a handy chart that breaks everything down.

For your free "Navigate Sales Diagnosis" go to:

http://www.ssnseminars.com/Sales-Coaching.aspx and click on the *chat live* button.

Also join our free e-zine at:

http://members.audiogenerator.com/info.asp?x=137686

Behavior Style	Approach	Presentation	Question
Fighter	• Jump right to the point • Give value statements immediately	• Talk about the bottom line • Be specific • Challenge them positively	• Answer *what* questions
Entertainer	• Begin with pleasantries • Build rapport • Drop names	• Be enthusiastic • Keep things fun • Use bullet points	• Answer *who* questions
Detective	• Be specific • State your objective • Be prepared to give details	• Use specifics • Use charts, graphs, and figures • Provide a lot of details	• Answer *why* questions
Counselor	• Take it slow • Talk in casual manner • Invite the team to presentation	• Make sure they understand product benefits • Seek their feedback and opinion • Be supportive and highlight benefits to team	• Answer *how* questions

Chapter 7

Navigate the Close

Closing is helping people get from point A to point B by providing a service that will help them reach their hopes and dreams in life faster

While the approach is probably the most important step and the presentation should be the shortest step, the closing is essential to securing the deal. You could find the right client, make a connection, sell that client on your product, and never reap the rewards if you don't close the deal. When people think of *closing*, they frequently associate the wrong meaning with the word. Some people think that closing is convincing people to do something that they don't want to do. In reality, closing is helping people get from point A to point B by providing a service that will help them reach their hopes and dreams in life faster.

What you need to realize is that the prospects you're talking to will end up at point B with or without you. The question is, will you be the one to help them get there? And can you provide such a superior service that you can help them get where they want to go faster?

By using the following closing techniques, you will help your clients live a better quality life and save yourself the frustration and anguish of hearing people tell you *maybe*.

> *It's easy to take a yes and you can live with a no,*
> *but it's the maybe that will kill you.*

As I mentioned earlier, **the art of the closing is all about navigating the fear of the buyer. When you learn the fears of people with different buying styles have, you will know how to navigate the close properly.** To recap: *Fighters fear losing control,* so you need to give them two positive choices. *Entertainers fear rejection and not having fun,* so you need to let them picture the fun they will have with your product or service. *Detectives fear being wrong,* so you should use logic to close the sale with them. *Counselors fear change,* so it's important to create a buying atmosphere and let them off the hook. As you've seen the right and wrong ways to approach people with the various buying behavior styles and present to people with the various buying behavior styles, now notice below the right and wrong ways to close people with the various buying behavior styles.

When to Adapt Your Selling Style

Now that you know the different buying behavior styles of individuals, you should be better prepared. Just as you should prepare four different presentations (or adapt your presentation to best fit the four different buying behavior styles), you should prepare four different closing techniques (or adapt your closing to the different behavior styles). Being prepared ahead of time will make everything go that much more smoothly when in the moment, and will allow you to roll with the punches more easily in those unpredictable moments. By the time you get to the closing step of the sales cycle, you should already be in the zone, having matched your selling style to their buying style. It should be second nature at the closing to continue with the same style. However, in the heat of the moment, just before the sale, it's easy to forget and lapse back into your natural selling style. It is important to stay focused and remain in the zone through the closing.

Closing Fighters

Let's first talk about the fear of a fighter. A fighter's main fear is losing control. Knowing that the fear of a fighter is losing control, whenever you're speaking with somebody who has that dominant buying behavior style, who tries to control the conversation and get straight to the point, the best way to close the deal is a technique called the choice of two positives. While a simple technique, with fighters *the choice of two positives* is very effective. You offer two positive solutions, and let them choose which one they prefer. For instance, if you're setting an appointment with a fighter, instead of saying, "I'll meet you Thursday at 4:00 at Starbucks," say, "What would be better for you, Tuesday or Thursday? Thursday, that's great! What would you prefer, 2:00 or 4:00? Four o'clock; all right. Where do you prefer to meet: Starbucks or Joe's Coffee? Okay, Starbucks, 4:00, Thursday." Let's see how this works in our scenario.

Role Play

Wrong: Richard Closing as a Detective

"Josh, do you have any questions about the statistics and data we have looked at so far?" Richard begins.

Josh replies, "Nope, no questions."

Richard continues, "As you can see in this pie chart, 27 percent of the investors saw a 15 percent ROI. Then over here on our analytical analysis chart, you can see by our proven track record over the course of the past ten years, we have out performed the competition."

Josh's eyes glaze over. "Can we just get to the bottom line? How much is it?"

"Well, statistics tell us that in different areas there are different prices."

Josh cuts him short. "I don't think I'm interested."

Right: Richard Adapts His Style

"So, Josh, which option did you like best, A or B?"

"B," Josh says.

"What was your favorite feature about option B?"

"The price!"

"Okay, well, if I'm reading you right (as Richard pulls out the contract), it seems like this is a fit and the bottom line seems to make sense. All I need to get you started is to know do you get your mail at your house or the post office?"

Giving fighters options that are positive gives them the impression that they're in control, but in reality, you're actually in control by giving the choice of two positives. You can do this all the way through the close, to where you could say, "What option do you like better? Option A or Option B?" They choose Option B, and you can go so far as to say, "Would you prefer to do credit card or check? Credit card—would you prefer to do Visa or MasterCard? Okay, would you rather start today or next week?" As long as you keep giving them control, they will like you and trust you. You will do more business with fighters by using the technique of the choice of two positives.

Closing Entertainers

The most effective way to bring entertainers to a point of decision is by dreaming with them. Help them see the big picture. Help them get excited and emotionally attached. That's the way that entertainers enjoy buying. A good technique to use on an entertainer is the crystal ball close. Hold out your hand as though you were holding a crystal ball and looking into the future. If you're selling a car, it might go something like this: "You know, Kyah, five years from now, what do you see yourself enjoying the most about this car? Do you see yourself with the convertible top down and your hair blowing in the wind going down the freeway? Do you see your friends piled in, jamming out to some tunes on this awesome Bose stereo system? What feature do you see that you'd enjoy the most?" With the crystal ball close, entertainers will imagine themselves in the picture that you painted for them, actually using your product or service. They'll decide to buy whatever it is you're showing them because you emotionally charged them. See how this can work in the scenario below.

Role Play

Right: Richard Closing as an Entertainer

"Well, Samantha, if you could look one year into the future, what gets you more excited about working with us? Is it that you will have one-on-one interaction with a personal consultant who will help hold you accountable to achieving your goals, or are you more excited about the social networking program that you will have access to?"

Wrong: Amy Not Adapting Her Counselor Style

"Well, Samantha. What do you think?"

Richard is an entertainer, so he is instinctively drawn to the big picture and seeing things as they could be. It would be easy for him to get Samantha emotionally charged, if he had already built good rapport and presented the product with vivid description. By the time he was ready to close, he already had her. The final step was getting Samantha to see herself using and enjoying the product. Amy on the other hand is a counselor. Selling to Samantha as a counselor had a negative effect because Amy used the worst close in the world the "what do you think" close. She was trying to make her feel comfortable and create a buying atmosphere during the close by asking that question, but all she needed to do was paint a satisfying picture of Samantha using the product in the future.

Being Navigated

One time I went into a retail store to buy a hat. The person working at the store was an undercover "Navigator" that I was unaware of. He walked up to me and said, "Hey, how's it going?"

I said, "Good," and he said, "That's great!" and then he walked off. That immediately got my attention because retailers usually walk up and say, "How may I help you?" Well, this gentleman didn't and he was probably one of the best salesmen I ever met because he knew how to "Navigate" the situation and then sell me.

He walked up to me about two minutes later and asked me, "Hey, man, so. . . what are you getting into this weekend? Do you have any big plans?"

I scratched my head and awkwardly replied, "Umm. . . I'm going out to the lake."

He quickly responded with, "The lake—that's awesome! Do you ever go skiing, knee boarding, or tubing?"

I said, "Sure, I do it all."

The "Navigator" salesman went on to ask, "Do you ever hang out on your dock after skiing all day?"

I replied, "Yes."

Then he said, "Do you drink Corona?"

Confused, I responded with, "I suppose so?" *I'm thinking, Man, this is weird; what's he been smoking, right?*

So he left again and came back about a minute later and said, "You've gotta check this out." By now, my curiosity's piqued, and I'm wondering what this guy's doing. He took me over to a shelf and showed me a pair of sandals. "Check this out," he said as he pulled a pair of sandals off the shelf. "Imagine this: Later on this weekend, you're out skiing all day, having fun on the lake. You get down to your dock and you're lying out in the sun, relaxing. You reach into the cooler to get your Corona when, all of a sudden, you realize that you left your bottle opener up at the cabin. Would that frustrate you?"

"Yes!" I blurted out.

"What if you had a pair of sandals with a bottle opener in them? Wouldn't that be pretty cool?"

"Yes!" I exclaimed again, more energized this time.

He flipped over the sandals he had in his hand and in the bottom of the sandal was a bottle opener. Being an entertainer, I bought it hook, line, and sinker. "Sold! This is amazing!" I took the sandals, put them on the register, and said, "I'll take them!" I didn't even ask how much they were. As I was shelling out my money to pay for these sandals that I did not need and totally forgetting about the hat that I came there to purchase, I realized that I had just been "Navigated" and I loved it!

Just remember, if you want to sell to an entertainer, paint a good picture and let him imagine actually having fun using the product and enjoying its benefits.

Closing Detectives

Detectives think logically. They don't buy into the crystal ball close, with its imaginative scenarios of enjoying the product or service in the future. Instead, a technique called the product/price/performance close (PPP close) works best for detectives. The PPP close is very logical and unemotional. In a peer-to-peer setting, detectives might be giving some kind of objection. Basically, you need to ask three easy questions: Do you like the product? Do you like the price? Do you like the performance? Of course, you'll need to ask these questions with context, such as:

"Well, Cindy, based on what I'm hearing you say, it seems that you like the product. What is *your favorite part* about the **product**?" She will then talk about the product. Then dig more deeply on that question and ask what is the main part of the product she will use the most. Let her talk about the things she would use. Then go on to the price.

"Now, Cindy, it seems like, *comparatively speaking*, you thought the **price** was reasonable. I remember you saying about the price, when it's compared to everything out on the market, you said that this was comparable, if not better. Do you agree that the price is fair?" Let her agree about the price. If you did a good job in delivering the price with a "price build up" such as we teach at our Success Starts Now!™ sales training conferences and personal sales coaching programs (www.ssnseminars.com) she will think the price is a fair price every time. Then the last part is the performance.

"Based on everything that I've shown you about the performance of the product, do you believe it will *get the same results* for you as it did for your friend who referred me to you? Do you *see the value* and that it is **something you will use**?" Let her agree with you that she sees herself using the product. After you have walked the detective through the steps in a logical way, you can look her in the eye and say, "You know, Cindy, this just seems to *makes sense*. If you like the product and you think the price is fair and you know you'll use it, this should be a *no-brainer*. It's just **logical** that we should move forward with this." When you can logically walk a detective through the process of the product, the price, and the performance, you will consistently and unemotionally be able to close the deal with her.

Let's take a look at how a poor exchange might go.

Role Play

Wrong: Richard Closing as an Entertainer

"Andy, if you could look into a crystal ball and see five years into the future, what do you see yourself enjoying the most? Would you be excited about having a big party in your dining room, or decorating your bedroom the way you've always wanted? Isn't this house absolutely exciting?"

Right: Richard Adapting His Style

"Do you have any questions about the statistics and data we have looked at so far, Andy?" Richard asks.

Andy replies, "Yes. What is the ROI?"

"As you can see in this pie chart," Richard explains, "27 percent of the investors saw a 15 percent ROI. Then over here on our analytical analysis chart, you can see by our proven track record over the course of the past ten years we have outperformed the competition."

"How does this compare to the competition?"

"Well, statistics tell us that different areas have different prices."

Andy responds, "This sounds interesting."

Then Richard proceeds to close with the PPP close. The PPP close is much more effective on detectives. It walks them through the steps and objections in a logical progression. It's organized, informative, and to the point. Just what detectives like. The first exchange in the role play was too much for Andy. Richard focused on the dreaminess of the product and didn't get to the fundamentals and details until too late. By then he had lost Andy. Remember, it's all about making a connection, not only in the first seven seconds but throughout the sales cycle.

Closing Counselors

Change is the greatest fear of counselors. What they want is a "steady Eddie," so don't ruffle their feathers. Downplay any benefits that would be a big change from their status quo. Demonstrate the selling points in such a way that they are great improvements with minor disruptions. The best close to use with a counselor is the walk-out close. This technique takes away the objection that they typically would give you at the end of a presentation and lets you use it to your advantage. It only works if it's in a group setting, but a group could simply mean two or more people. If the decision-maker in the group is a counselor, when you finish your presentation, look at the counselor and say, "You know, Don, *if I'm reading you right*, you seem to think this is a *pretty good idea*. Based on what I'm hearing, everyone seems to like the benefits and features. Jan, what *seemed to resonate* with you in the presentation? (Jan responds) Okay, and John, what was *your favorite part*? (John tells his favorite part) Great! Well as a *professional courtesy* to you and the group, I want to make sure that you have an opportunity to discuss it without me in the room. I'm going to step out for about five minutes. The only favor that I ask is that when I return you give me a *thumbs-up or a thumbs-down*. We have covered all of the details about the product, so *by this point you guys should know if this is for you or not*." **It is key that you say this before you leave.** Then you leave for five minutes. When you come back, you'll come back into a much better situation. It is painful when they have to ask you to step out of the room without your setting up the walk-out close—it usually sounds something like this, "You know, Dustin, this really sounds great but we need to think this over and talk about it. Could you step out of the room for five minutes, or even better could you just come back tomorrow and we will have our decision?"—then the odds of your actually closing the deal that day go down very dramatically.

The walk-out close is perfect for groups and ideal for counselors, as you've seen above. When an fighter closes to a counselor without adapting his or her style, it usually has a negative effect, as seen below.

Role Play

Wrong: Richard Closing as a Fighter

"All right, Lisa. Everything looks like you're in. So all I need is for you to fill out this contract and sign right here."

Lisa replies, "I really need to think about this."

"What is there to think about?" counters Richard. "Just sign right here."

"No," Lisa responds, "I think we are fine with what we've got."

Right: **Richard Adapting His Style**

"Well, if I'm reading everyone right, it seems like we are all on the same page," Richard begins. "John, you were saying you really liked option A, and Mary, you said you really appreciate the money back guarantee." Richard continues with the walk-out close. "As a professional courtesy to all of you, I'm going to step out of the room for a couple of minutes to make sure you guys can discuss this and make sure you all feel good about this decision. Since we have already gone through all of the details, and I've shown you everything there is to think about, the only favor that I ask is when I come back in, just let me know one way or another about how you all want to proceed. Does that sound fair?"

Some people don't like to sell to counselors because they usually make decisions based on how the group feels. Groups can be difficult if not handled properly, because they usually play off each other and end up needing to "get back to you" with an answer. Since 75 percent of sales happen the same day you present the benefits and price structure (which should take someone over the buying line) and only 25 percent come from a follow-up call or meeting, you can see why it's so important to close the first time you take someone over the buying line. The walk-out close greatly improves your chances of closing to a counselor on the first meeting.

Adapting to Fighters

Do . . .

- Offer them a choice between two positives.
- Let them feel as though they are in control.
- Answer their *what* questions.

Don't . . .

- Be vague about particulars.
- Give them big picture ideas.
- Beat around the bush.

Adapting to Entertainers

Do . . .

- Begin with pleasantries.
- Build rapport.
- Be enthusiastic and energetic, complimenting and encouraging.
- Sell the big picture with lots of sizzle.
- Ask their opinions and dream with them.
- Keep things fun by using stories and testimonials.
- Provide bullet point brochure to help with retention.
- Drop names of people they know.
- Answer their *who* questions.

Don't . . .

- Bore them with details.
- Come on too strong at first.
- Give them too many facts and figures.

Adapting to Detectives

Do . . .

- Be prepared to give details.
- Use charts, graphs, and figures.
- Be specific and remain objective and not overly emotional.
- Match their controlled tone of voice.
- Answer their *why* questions.

Don't . . .

- Offer your opinion.
- Give big picture generalizations.
- Force a quick decision. Allow them "think time."
- Be vague about expectations or fail to follow through.

Adapting to Counselors

Do . . .

- Take it more slowly with them.
- Tone it down and speak in a casual, personal manner.
- Make sure they understand product benefits.
- Ask for their opinion.
- Be supportive and take charge gradually.
- Discuss how the team will benefit.
- Answer their *how* questions.

Don't . . .

- Be demanding or force quick decisions.

Conclusion

So, in summary, for how to close the four different behavior styles, let me give you a quick synopsis. For fighters, alleviate their fear of loss of control by giving them a choice of two positives. For entertainers, calm their fear of rejection and not having fun by exciting them with the crystal ball close. For detectives, dampen their fear of being wrong by logically walking them through the PPP (product/price/performance) close. For counselors, reduce their fear of change by including the entire team with the walk-out close. Those are the four closing techniques for the different behavior styles.

For your free "Navigate Sales Diagnosis" go to:
http://www.ssnseminars.com/Sales-Coaching.aspx and click on the *chat live* button.
Also join our free e-zine at:
http://members.audiogenerator.com/info.asp?x=137686

Behavior Style	Approach	Presentation	Close	Question
Fighter	• Jump right in with the reason you're calling • Give value statements immediately	• Be specific • Talk about the bottom line • Challenge them positively	• Offer them choices • Make them feel in control • Use the choice of two positives close	• Answer *what* questions
Entertainer	• Begin with pleasantries • Build rapport • Drop names	• Be enthusiastic • Keep things fun • Use bullet points	• Help them get excited • Dream with them • Paint a positive picture • Use the crystal ball close	• Answer *who* questions
Detective	• Be specific • State your objective • Be prepared to give details	• Use specifics • Use charts, graphs, and figures • Provide a lot of details	• Walk them through logically • Give them all the benefits • Use the PPP close	• Answer *why* questions
Counselor	• Take it slow • Talk in casual manner • Invite the team to presentation	• Make sure they understand product benefits • Seek their feedback and opinion • Be supportive and highlight benefits to team	• Close with them in a group • Give them time to decide alone • Use the walk-out close	• Answer *how* questions

Chapter 8

It's Time to Have Some Fun

Do unto others as they would have
done unto themselves.

You have just read a lot of material about reading people and adapting to their buying behavior styles. No doubt you are itching to pick up the phone, walk through your office, or run over to the area with the most people nearby and start "Navigating"! Now that you're aware of the Navigate principles and techniques, you will never be bored again. You can have fun reading people from afar while honing your skills. Whether you are reading faces in a crowded restaurant, identifying buying behavior style by assessing someone's attire in an airport while waiting for your plane, or most importantly, identifying and adapting to someone's buying behavior style in person or over the phone to set an appointment and win the business, you now can read people and change your style in order to best connect with them emotionally.

As a side note, these Navigate principles can be used in many more situations than just selling. These are universal principles that translate to all relationships and general conversations. If you find that you are always fighting with your spouse, your kids, or your in-laws, it may be because your buying and selling behavior styles don't match. You can "Navigate" them and adapt your style to better relate to them. It is about understanding human psychology and being able to adapt to all kinds of situations and in all kinds of different situations.

Navigate principles can be used in many more situations than just selling. These are universal principles that translate to all relationships and general conversations.

The ability to "Navigate" someone is a powerful tool. You have the tools now to begin to exhibit a certain power of communication that will influence people. With that power comes the awesome responsibility to use your skills wisely. Now that you have been armed with the Navigate technology, you must use it for good, not evil. This sounds like a joke, but I'm being perfectly serious. These techniques will work, and the temptation will be there to manipulate and take advantage of other people who don't need or want your services. Here is a quote that will throw you for a loop: "the Golden Rule doesn't apply to sales". In a sense that is true, because we shouldn't always sell to others as we would have them sell to us. However, at a much more important level, the Golden Rule is most important in the field of sales. Because professional salespeople are more skilled than the average person at reading people and connecting with them, touching their hot buttons, we have a greater responsibility not to abuse people. I described in Chapter 7 the story of my having been "Navigated" when trying to buy a hat. I ended up walking out of the store with a pair of sandals that I didn't think I needed. I was certainly impressed by the salesman's ability to read me like a book and to find the need that I didn't even know I had. However, convincing people to buy something they don't want or can't afford can have a significantly negative impact. We are all trained to up-sell to get the most out of a sale, and with the Navigate tools, you will have the skills to sell all different kinds of people on the added benefits of a product or service. However, I would be remiss if I didn't encourage you to be honest and considerate when selling to people (or businesses) who may not be able to afford your product or service or the extras that you may want to sell. You are there to serve customers by selling them what they need and keeping them from buying something they don't need or can't afford. It's about building a relationship, not just making a sale.

This is a true story. One time a sales rep for our professional sales training division was doing an "Immediate Results" sales training workshop as a way of selling tickets to one of our large sales training conferences. At the conclusion of the training session, the general manager of the company stood up and said, "This looks great; I think we all like what you guys are offering, and it looks like everyone is interested in going. Here is my company credit card. Go ahead and sign us up for fifteen VIP tickets." Then the general manager excused himself from the room and went to his next meeting. The rep got excited at the opportunity to close a sale for over six thousand dollars and started to write up the order. As he was writing up the sale, a couple of the sales managers began discussing whether they could actually attend the conference, and if they actually wanted their whole sales team to attend. They came to the conclusion that instead of the fifteen tickets, they wanted to get just seven tickets—less than half of what the general manager had said he wanted to purchase! The sales rep smiled and "Navigated" the situation. He came to find out that the managers just did not want to be excessive, and they were trying to make the big man proud. (At this point, the rep should have just signed up the seven people and been happy with helping out the team.) Instead of giving them what they wanted, however, he made the mistake of being greedy, and knowing that he had the skill set to close more tickets, he took the registration forms over to the general manager, adapted his selling style to that of a counselor, and let him know that his team just wanted to make sure that he felt like they weren't being excessive. The rep wanted the general manager to make sure he felt safe with the decision to send fifteen people to the event. He told the GM, "Your managers said that seven of them definitely want to attend, but I'm sure you have several team members who were not in attendance today that you would want to make sure we took care of and didn't leave out. Would you like for me to go ahead and throw just two or three more tickets on this order to make sure we get everyone who should be going?" The general manager said, "Sure, that sounds fine." The next week the sales trainer received a call from the general manager saying that he thought the training session was great and his team was excited to go. However, his team felt like they were being taken advantage of. After clearly being told that they wanted to send only seven people, the rep went directly to the boss and signed up three more. They canceled the entire order!

The sad part to this story is that I was that young professional sales rep! I was actually doing the workshop as a training session for one of our new sales reps, and I was "showing her the ropes." What a great example that was! I felt so terrible I didn't know what to say to the general manager when I went back to the office to try to salvage the sale. But through that experience I learned a valuable lesson: always put your customer's best interest first. Never sell something to someone just because you can. Always identify the need, and make sure he or she is qualified to buy your service or product.

When I first started out in sales, I was all about me. My attitude was one of trying at all costs to earn as much money as I could as fast as I could. I worked over eighty hours a week during the summers while I was in college, and then two to three jobs while going to school. I was living out that old saying, "Work hard and play hard." My personal relationships suffered and, worst of all, I was forming habits that weren't conducive to building lasting relationships with my customers. I told myself that I was meeting their needs, but in reality I didn't care about them at all. I was number one in my life. Because I was calling on so many people a day, none of them were repeat customers. Between the ages of sixteen and twenty-two, I was hell on wheels. You name it and I did it. The interesting thing about my trip to the wild side was that every morning I woke up and knew that the person I was *being* was not the person I wanted to *become*. I had dreams and aspirations of becoming a respected and successful entrepreneur, and the actions and behaviors I was displaying were not at all in line with who I wanted to become. Then I started dating Kyah, my angel, now my wife, and one day I was pretty down in the dumps—perhaps the lowest point of my life. I tried to logically think myself into a good mood by using positive self- talk and reminding myself of all my great accomplishments. After all, just three months earlier I had broken the all-time sales record for The Southwestern Company; I had been a college athlete; I had a beautiful girlfriend; blah, blah, blah. None of those worldly accomplishments satisfied the hole that I felt inside myself. And I was living a self-destructive lifestyle and was living for the moment, not for the future.

The reason I call Kyah my angel is because of what she asked me on the day I was at my lowest. She asked, "Do you have any positive mentors or friends that you hang out with who are doing what you want to do or become?" And that is when it hit me. I knew that I wanted to be a Christian leader, upstanding business owner, and eventually a great husband and father. But up to that point in my life, I had not hung out with or spent much time with anyone who had those same values and beliefs. The old saying that "you are only as successful as your five best friends" is so true, and that was one of the things I needed to change: my friends. First, though, I needed to ask for forgiveness from all those close to me for hurting them with my selfishness. Once I got everything in order with God, the next thing I did was start hanging out with other successful Christian business owners. I came to realize that life was about so much more than just making money. It was about cultivating relationships, and ultimately your relationship with Jesus Christ. We most certainly *are* to apply the Golden Rule to sales as to every other area of our lives. We should be selling to people as though they were our fathers or mothers, our sons or daughters, even as though they were us. Would you want your son or daughter to be taken advantage of? Before I rededicated my life to Jesus Christ, I was using all my talent and ability to influence people for my own selfish gain. Once I came to realize that the world did not revolve around me and that the right thing to do is to love your neighbor as yourself, my world changed in ways I never thought possible. By being more concerned about the customer than whether I made the sale or not, God actually gave me *more* success in my career than I had ever had before.

So, go out and practice what you have learned with Navigate and have fun doing it. But remember to apply Navigate to the Golden Rule and treat other people the way they would like to be treated.

God bless!

For your free "Navigate Sales Diagnosis" go to:
http://www.ssnseminars.com/Sales-Coaching.aspx and click on the *chat live* button.
Also join our free e-zine at:
http://members.audiogenerator.com/info.asp?x=137686